Autumn Bouquet

PATCHWORK AND APPLIQUÉ QUILTS
FROM REPRODUCTION PRINTS

SHARON KEIGHTLEY

Martingale
Create with Confidence

Autumn Bouquet: Patchwork and Appliqué Quilts from Reproduction Prints
© 2019 by Sharon Keightley

Martingale®
19021 120th Ave. NE, Ste. 102
Bothell, WA 98011-9511 USA
ShopMartingale.com

Printed in China
24 23 22 21 20 19   8 7 6 5 4 3 2 1

Library of Congress Cataloging-in-Publication Data is available upon request.

ISBN: 978-1-68356-018-0

MISSION STATEMENT

We empower makers who use fabric and yarn to make life more enjoyable.

CREDITS

PUBLISHER AND
CHIEF VISIONARY OFFICER
Jennifer Erbe Keltner

CONTENT DIRECTOR
Karen Costello Soltys

MANAGING EDITOR
Tina Cook

ACQUISITIONS AND
DEVELOPMENT EDITOR
Laurie Baker

TECHNICAL EDITOR
Nancy Mahoney

COPY EDITOR
Melissa Bryan

DESIGN MANAGER
Adrienne Smitke

PRODUCTION MANAGER
Regina Girard

INTERIOR DESIGNER
Angie Hoogensen

STUDIO PHOTOGRAPHER
Brent Kane

LOCATION PHOTOGRAPHER
Adam Albright

ILLUSTRATOR
Sandy Loi

DEDICATION

To my late mother, who always encouraged me, teaching me the skills and passing on her passion for sewing. Her favorite saying was "where there is a will, there is a way." I am truly grateful to my husband, Malcolm; my sons, Derek and Peter; and their partners, Megan and Holly, for their never-ending love and their support of my quilting addiction.

Contents

Introduction

Quilts have always held a strong fascination for me. I think of quilts as pieces of fabric bound together with love, telling stories of the past and future, handed down from generation to generation and withstanding the boundaries of time. The quilts you see in this book represent part of my journey as a quiltmaker, showing my strong affection for reproduction fabrics and antique quilts. Over time, I've found pleasure in using the fabrics I love to create my own style.

Most of the quilts include pieced blocks plus appliqué, which has become one of my favorite parts of the quiltmaking process. I enjoy working with a variety of appliqué methods to find the one that suits the style of each quilt, tweaking each part to get the look I'm after.

I love the whole process of making a quilt, from choosing the fabrics and design to piecing the blocks, stitching the appliqués, and quilting the layers together. My appliqué tips have been gathered through trial and error. Using invaluable tools and notions has made the journey easier and more enjoyable. I look forward to sharing all I've learned and hope you enjoy making your own versions of the quilts in this book.

Rose of Thorns

A dark rose among thorny leaves holds a special beauty. While the layers of the traditional rose motif add depth to the design, they're easy to stitch as layered units prior to appliquéing the rose to the quilt top.

FINISHED QUILT: 22½" × 22½" ◆ **FINISHED CENTER BLOCK:** 14" × 14"

Materials

Yardage is based on 42"-wide fabric. Fat eighths measure 9" × 21". Fat quarters measure 18" × 21".

1 fat quarter of beige print for appliqué background

1 fat eighth *each* of yellow print, teal stripe, olive print, brown plaid, and cream stripe for appliqués

1 fat quarter of green check for flying-geese units and outer border

1 fat quarter *total* of assorted pink and other light prints for flying-geese and square-in-a-square units (collectively referred to as "pink")*

1 fat quarter *total* of assorted plum prints for flying-geese units and appliqué

½ yard of dark plum print for square-in-a-square units, rose appliqué, and binding

¾ yard of fabric for backing

27" × 27" piece of batting

Wash-away appliqué paper

I used rose, tan, and green prints, as well as the green check in the outer border for the flying-geese units.

Cutting

All measurements include ¼" seam allowances.

From the beige print, cut:
1 square, 16" × 16"

From the green check, cut:
4 strips, 2½" × 18½"

From the assorted pink prints and leftover green check, cut a *total* of:
72 squares, 1⅞" × 1⅞"; cut 8 of the squares in half diagonally to yield 16 triangles

From the assorted plum prints, cut a *total* of:
16 squares, 3¼" × 3¼"

From the dark plum print, cut:
3 strips, 2¼" × 42"
4 squares, 1⅞" × 1⅞"

Appliquéing the Center Block

1 Using the patterns on pages 10 and 11 and referring to "Method 2: Wash-Away Appliqué Paper" on page 75, prepare four yellow flower centers, four teal stripe flowers, four olive leaves, one dark plum rose, one brown plaid large circle, one cream stripe medium circle, and one plum print small circle.

2 Referring to "Building Appliqué Units" on page 78, construct the center rose shape.

3 Fold the beige square in half diagonally in both directions and crease to create centering lines. Referring to the appliqué placement diagram on page 8, position the rose in the center of the square. Position a flower and then a flower center on each diagonal crease. Tuck the stem end of each flower under the rose. Position a leaf between each flower. Stitch in place referring to "Stitching the Appliqués" on page 78.

Make It Easy

Using appliqué method 2 (page 75) to prepare the leaves makes it quite easy to turn the thorny edges. The appliqué shapes can be layered and basted all at once, and then stitched in place.

4 Trim the appliquéd block to measure 14½" square, keeping the design centered.

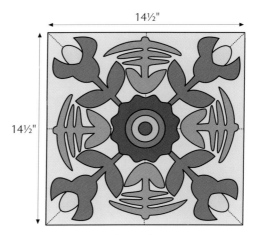

14½"

14½"

Appliqué placement

Making the Flying-Geese Border

Press all seam allowances in the direction indicated by the arrows.

1 Draw a diagonal line from corner to corner on the wrong side of the pink and green check 1⅞" squares. Align two marked squares on opposite corners of a plum 3¼" square, right sides together. Stitch ¼" from both sides of the line. Cut apart on the marked line.

2 Align a marked square on the remaining corner of each unit and sew ¼" from both sides of the line. Cut on the marked lines and press to make four identical flying-geese units measuring 1½" × 2½", including seam allowances. Make a total of 64 units.

Make 64 units,
1½" × 2½".

3 Join 14 flying-geese units to make a border strip measuring 2½" × 14½", including seam allowances. Make two for the side borders. Join 18 flying-geese units to make a border strip measuring 2½" × 18½", including seam allowances. Make two for the top and bottom borders.

Make 2 side borders,
2½" × 14½".

Make 2 top/bottom borders,
2½" × 18½".

Assembling the Quilt Top

1 Sew the border strips to opposite sides of the quilt top and then to the top and bottom, making sure to orient them as shown in the quilt assembly diagram below. The quilt top should measure 18½" square, including seam allowances.

2 Fold a dark plum square in half vertically and horizontally, and lightly crease to mark the center on each side. Fold four pink triangles in half, and lightly crease to mark the center of the long side. Sew triangles to opposite sides of the square, matching the center creases. Sew triangles to the remaining sides of the square to make a square-in-a-square unit measuring 2½" square, including seam allowances. Make four units.

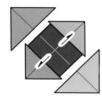

Make 4 units,
2½" × 2½".

3 Sew green check 18½"-long strips to opposite sides of the quilt center.

4 Sew square-in-a-square units to each end of the remaining green check strips. Sew these strips to the top and bottom of the quilt top. The quilt top should measure 22½" square.

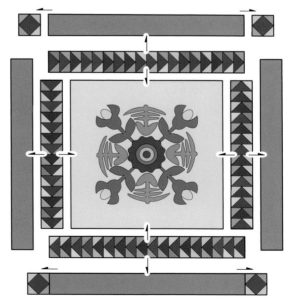

Quilt assembly

Finishing the Quilt

For more details on the following finishing steps, visit ShopMartingale.com/HowtoQuilt for free downloadable information.

1 Layer the quilt top with batting and backing; baste the layers together.

2 Quilt by hand or machine. The quilt shown is machine quilted in the ditch and then echo quilted in the quilt center. The flying-geese border is quilted with curvy triangles, and the outer border features a pumpkin seed design.

3 Using the dark plum 2¼"-wide strips, make binding and then attach the binding to the quilt.

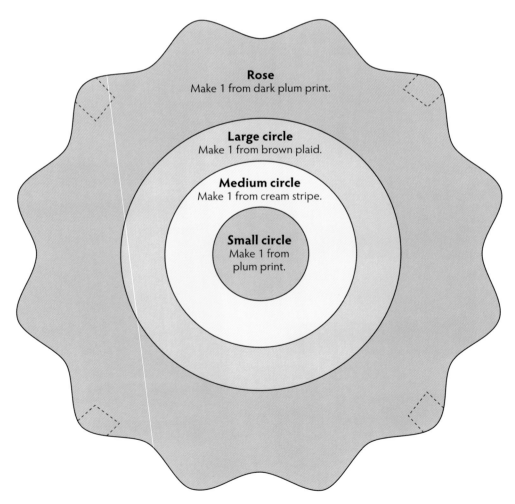

Rose
Make 1 from dark plum print.

Large circle
Make 1 from brown plaid.

Medium circle
Make 1 from cream stripe.

Small circle
Make 1 from plum print.

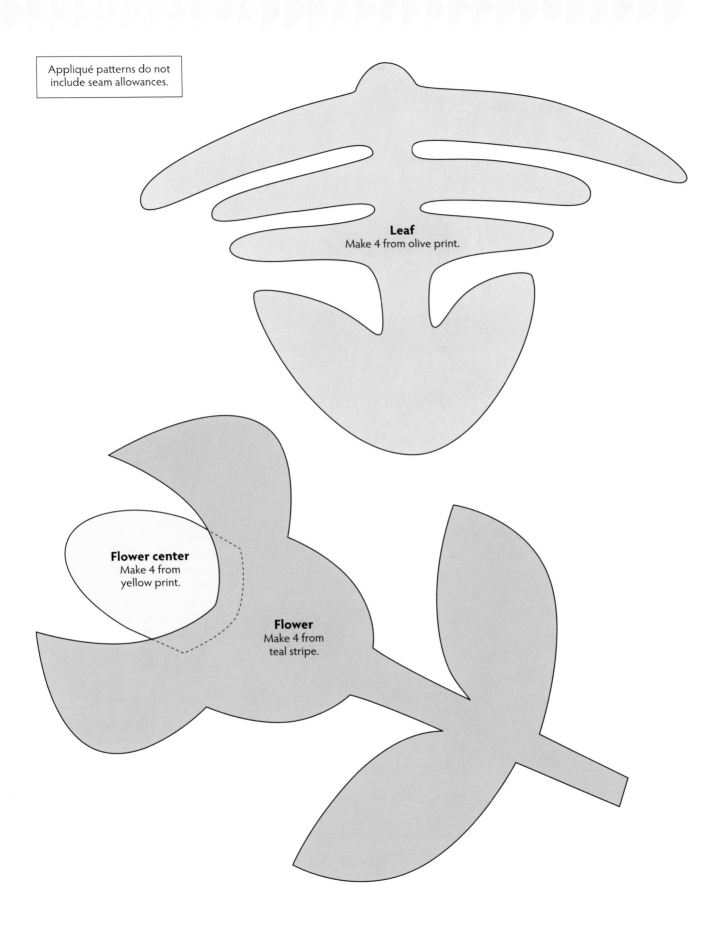

Appliqué patterns do not include seam allowances.

Leaf
Make 4 from olive print.

Flower center
Make 4 from yellow print.

Flower
Make 4 from teal stripe.

Treasures from the Scrap Bin

Little scraps of leftover fabrics are like treasures in an old chest just waiting to be discovered. Gather your scraps and sew them together with love to make a cherished quilt that will endure through time.

FINISHED QUILT: 21¼" × 34" ◆ **FINISHED BLOCK:** 3" × 3"

Materials

Yardage is based on 42"-wide fabric. Fat eighths measure 9" × 21". Fat quarters measure 18" × 21".

1 yard *total* of assorted light prints for blocks and outer border

½ yard *total* of assorted medium to dark prints for blocks, setting triangles, and inner border (collectively referred to as "dark")

1 fat quarter *each* of 2 beige prints for setting blocks

1 fat quarter *total* of assorted green prints for leaves

1 fat quarter *total* of assorted red, blue, brown, gold, and black prints for flowers

1 fat eighth of black floral for flowerpots

1 fat eighth of tan print for vines

¼ yard of red diagonal stripe for binding

¾ yard of fabric for backing

26" × 38" piece of batting

Freezer paper

¼" bias-tape maker

Cutting

All measurements include ¼" seam allowances.

From the light prints, cut a *total* of:
4 squares, 3½" × 3½"
18 sets of 2 matching squares, 2" × 2" (36 total)
72 squares, 1½" × 1½"
Approximately 85 strips, 1⅛" to 1⅞" × 3½"

From the dark prints, cut a *total* of:
2 strips, 1½" × 26"
2 strips, 1½" × 15¼"
3 squares, 6" × 6"; cut the squares into quarters diagonally to yield 12 side triangles (2 are extra)
2 squares, 3" × 3"; cut the squares in half diagonally to yield 4 corner triangles
18 sets of 2 matching squares, 2" × 2" (36 total)
18 squares, 1½" × 1½"

From *each* of the beige prints, cut:
3 squares, 6" × 6"; cut the squares into quarters diagonally to yield 12 triangles (24 total)

From the tan print, cut on the *bias*:
4 strips, ½" × 12"
4 strips, ½" × 7½"

From the red diagonal stripe, cut:
3 strips, 2¼" × 42"

Making the Shoofly Blocks

Press all seam allowances in the direction indicated by the arrows.

1 Draw a diagonal line from corner to corner on the wrong side of the light 2" squares. Layer a marked square on a dark 2" square, right sides together. Sew ¼" from both sides of the drawn line. Cut the unit apart on the marked line to make two half-square-triangle units. Trim the units to measure 1½" square, including seam allowances. Make 18 sets of four matching units (72 units total).

Make 72 units.

2 Lay out four light 1½" squares, four matching half-square-triangle units, and one dark 1½" square in three rows. Sew the squares and units together in rows. Join the rows to make a Shoofly block measuring 3½" square, including seam allowances. Make 18 blocks.

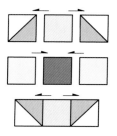

Make 18 blocks,
3½" × 3½".

Assembling the Quilt Top

1 Sew unmatched beige triangles together in pairs to make 10 Triangle blocks as shown. Trim the blocks to measure 3½" square, including seam allowances. You'll have two triangles from each print left over to use in the next step.

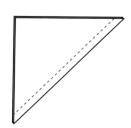

Make 10 blocks.

2 Lay out the Shoofly blocks, Triangle blocks, remaining beige triangles, dark side triangles, and dark corner triangles in diagonal rows as shown in the quilt assembly diagram. Sew the blocks and side triangles together in rows. Join the rows, adding the corner triangles last, to make the quilt-top center.

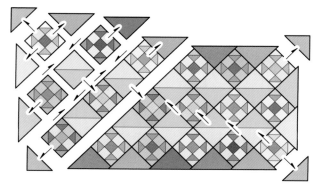

Quilt assembly

3 Trim and square up the quilt top, making sure to leave ¼" beyond the points of all the blocks for seam allowances. The quilt top should measure 13¼" × 26", including seam allowances.

Trim ¼" from point.

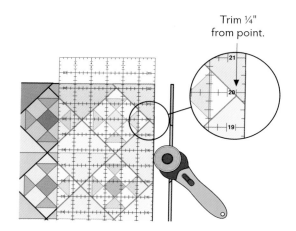

4 Sew the dark 1½" × 26" strips to the long edges of the quilt-top center. Sew the dark 1½" × 15¼" strips to the short edges of the quilt top.

5 Randomly join light 3½"-long strips along their long edges to make two 3½" × 28" border strips for the top and bottom borders.

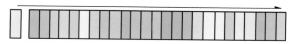

Make 2 top/bottom borders, 3½" × 28".

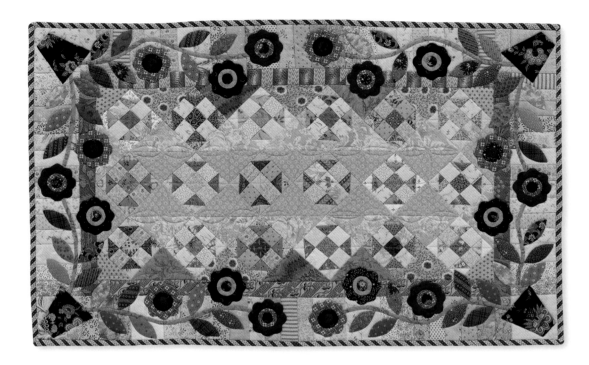

6 Randomly join light 3½"-long strips along their long edges to make a border strip measuring 3½" × 15¼", including seam allowances. Sew a light 3½" square to each end. Make two for the side borders.

Make 2 side borders, 3½" × 21¼".

7 Sew the 28"-long strips to the top and bottom of the quilt top. Sew the 21¼"-long strips to the sides of the quilt top. The quilt top should measure 21¼" × 34". Stay stitch ⅛" around the perimeter of the quilt top to stabilize the seams prior to appliqué.

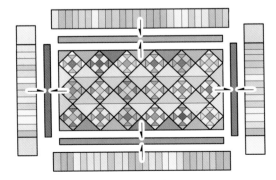

Adding borders

Appliquéing the Border

1 Using the patterns on page 16 and referring to "Method 1: Freezer Paper" on page 72, prepare 18 assorted red, blue, brown, gold, and black flowers, four black floral flowerpots, and 48 green leaves.

2 Referring to "Preparing Stems and Vines" on page 75, use the bias-tape maker and the tan strips to prepare four ¼" × 12" vines and four ¼" × 7½" vines.

3 Refer to the photo above and the appliqué placement diagram on page 16 as needed. On one short end of the quilt top, position a flowerpot in each corner of the outer border. Using two short vines, tuck one end under the flowerpot, and then curve each vine toward the center of the quilt's short end. Using two long vines, tuck one end under the flowerpot, and then curve each vine toward the center of the long side. Place a flower over the end of each long vine. Position one flower in the center of the short end, on top of both vine ends. Place two additional flowers along each long vine and one along each short vine. Position seven leaves along each long vine and five leaves along each short vine. The two groups of appliqués should be mirror images of each

15

other. Repeat to add appliqués to the other short end of the quilt top. Stitch the appliqués in place referring to "Stitching the Appliqués" on page 78.

Appliqué placement

Finishing the Quilt

For more details on the following finishing steps, visit ShopMartingale.com/HowtoQuilt for free downloadable information.

1 Layer the quilt top with batting and backing; baste the layers together.

2 Quilt by hand or machine. The quilt shown is machine stitched in the ditch. Straight lines are quilted in the Shoofly blocks and a pumpkin seed design is used in the Triangle blocks.

3 Using the red stripe 2¼"-wide strips, make binding and then attach the binding to the quilt.

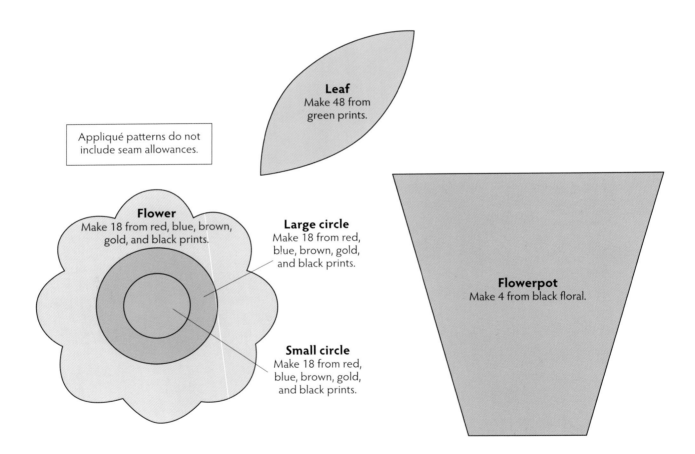

Leaf
Make 48 from green prints.

Appliqué patterns do not include seam allowances.

Flower
Make 18 from red, blue, brown, gold, and black prints.

Large circle
Make 18 from red, blue, brown, gold, and black prints.

Small circle
Make 18 from red, blue, brown, gold, and black prints.

Flowerpot
Make 4 from black floral.

Holly's Garden

Spring is in the air, with beautiful yellow, pink, and red blooms bursting to life everywhere you look in Holly's Garden. This charming quilt is like a fresh spring breeze for your home.

FINISHED QUILT: 22½" × 22½" ◆ **FINISHED CENTER BLOCK:** 10" × 10"

Materials

Yardage is based on 42"-wide fabric. Fat eighths measure 9" × 21".

11½" × 11½" square of light print for appliqué background

4 squares, 3" × 3" *each,* of assorted yellow prints for inner petals

8 squares, 3" × 3" *each,* of assorted green prints for leaves

2" × 3" rectangle of brown print for stems

16 rectangles, 4" × 5" *each,* of assorted light prints for pieced border

5 fat eighths of assorted blue prints for pieced border and flower buds

4 fat eighths of assorted pink prints for pieced border, corner blocks, bud centers, and flower center

4 fat eighths of assorted red prints for corner blocks and outer petals

4 fat eighths of assorted gold prints for middle border

¼ yard of red floral for outer border

¼ yard of gold floral for binding

¾ yard of fabric for backing

27" × 27" piece of batting

Wash-away appliqué paper

¼" bias-tape maker

Cutting

All measurements include ¼" seam allowances.

From the brown print, cut:
4 strips, ½" × 3"

From *each* light print rectangle, cut:
6 squares, 1½" × 1½" (96 total)

From *each* blue print, cut:
4 squares, 2½" × 2½" (20 total)

From *each* pink print, cut:
1 square, 4½" × 4½" (4 total)
1 square, 2½" × 2½" (4 total)

From *each* red print, cut:
4 squares, 2½" × 2½" (16 total)

From *each* gold print, cut:
1 strip, 1½" × 14½" (4 total)

From the red floral, cut:
4 strips, 3½" × 14½"

From the gold floral, cut:
3 strips, 2¼" × 42"

Appliquéing the Center Block

1 Using the patterns on page 21 and referring to "Method 2: Wash-Away Appliqué Paper" on page 75, prepare four yellow inner petals, four red outer petals, eight green leaves, four blue flower buds, four pink bud centers, and one pink flower center.

2 Referring to "Preparing Stems and Vines" on page 75, use the bias-tape maker and the brown strips to prepare four ¼" × 3" stems.

3 Fold the light 11½" square in half diagonally in both directions and lightly crease to establish centering lines. Referring to the appliqué placement diagram, position a flower bud in each corner of the square and then place a bud center on top of each bud. Using the creases as a guide, tuck one end of a stem under each flower bud, and place one leaf and one reversed leaf beside the stem. Position an outer petal at the bottom of each stem, tucking the stem under the petal. Place the inner petals in the center of the outer petals, with the sides touching. Place the flower center in the middle of the inner petals. Stitch the appliqués in place, referring to "Stitching the Appliqués" on page 78.

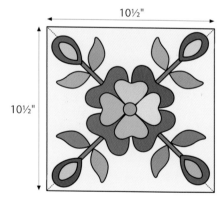

10½"

10½"

Appliqué placement

4 Trim the appliquéd block to measure 10½" square, keeping the design centered.

Making the Pieced Border

Press all seam allowances in the direction indicated by the arrows.

1 Draw a diagonal line from corner to corner on the wrong side of the light 1½" squares. Place marked squares on diagonally opposite corners of a blue square, right sides together with the marked lines oriented as shown. Sew on the marked lines. Trim the excess corner fabric ¼" from the stitched line. Repeat to sew marked squares on the remaining two corners to make a square-in-a-square unit measuring 2½" square, including seam allowances. Make 20 units. In the same way, use the remaining marked squares and the pink 2½" squares to make four units.

Make 20 units, 2½" × 2½".

Make 4 units, 2½" × 2½".

Assembling the Quilt Top

2 Join five blue units to make a border strip measuring 2½" × 10½", including seam allowances. Make two for the side borders. Make two more strips in the same way, and add a pink unit to each end to complete the top and bottom borders. These strips should measure 2½" × 14½", including seam allowances.

1 Using the red 2½" squares and the pink 4½" squares, repeat step 1 of "Making the Pieced Border" (page 19) to make four corner blocks measuring 4½" square, including seam allowances.

Make 2 side borders,
2½" × 10½".

Make 4 units,
4½" × 4½".

Make 2 top/bottom borders,
2½" × 14½".

Autumn Bouquet

2 Sew a gold print strip to a red floral strip to make an outer-border strip measuring 4½" × 14½", including seam allowances. Make four strips.

Make 4 strips, 4½" × 14½".

3 Sew the pieced side borders to opposite sides of the center block as shown in the quilt assembly diagram below. Sew the top and bottom pieced borders to the quilt top. The quilt top should measure 14½" square, including seam allowances.

4 Sew outer-border strips to opposite sides of the quilt top. Sew corner blocks to each end of the remaining outer-border strips, and sew these strips to the top and bottom of the quilt top. The quilt top should measure 22½" square.

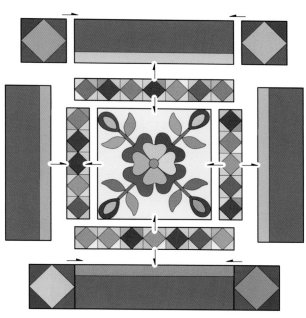

Quilt assembly

Finishing the Quilt

For more details on the following finishing steps, visit ShopMartingale.com/HowtoQuilt for free downloadable information.

1 Layer the quilt top with batting and backing; baste the layers together.

2 Quilt by hand or machine. The quilt shown is machine quilted in the ditch along the seamlines and around the appliqué shapes, with echo quilting in the background of the center block. Curved triangles are quilted in the pieced border and a scroll design is added throughout the gold border. The outer border features a diamond grid design, with a pumpkin seed motif in the corner blocks.

3 Using the gold floral 2¼"-wide strips, make binding and then attach the binding to the quilt.

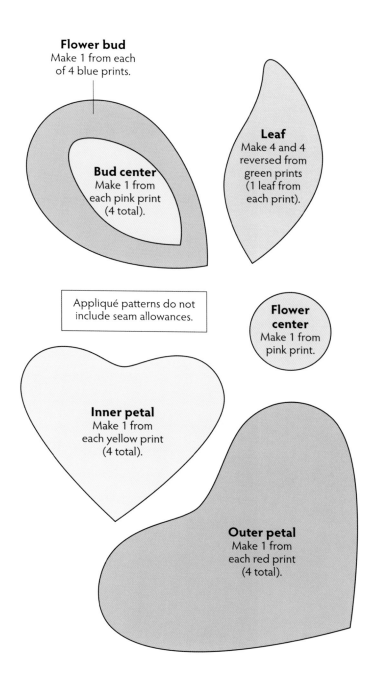

Flower bud
Make 1 from each of 4 blue prints.

Bud center
Make 1 from each pink print (4 total).

Leaf
Make 4 and 4 reversed from green prints (1 leaf from each print).

Appliqué patterns do not include seam allowances.

Flower center
Make 1 from pink print.

Inner petal
Make 1 from each yellow print (4 total).

Outer petal
Make 1 from each red print (4 total).

My Little Boho

The blend of fabrics and the mix of colors give this quilt a Bohemian look—hence its name. I had lots of fun selecting fabrics and playing with my favorite prints. It's always such a delight to see the finished look.

FINISHED QUILT: 22½" × 22½" ◆ **FINISHED CENTER BLOCK:** 12" × 12"

Materials

Yardage is based on 42"-wide fabric. Fat eighths measure 9" × 21".

6 fat eighths of assorted light prints for block

4 fat eighths of assorted green prints for block

2 squares, 5" × 5" *each,* of different dark brown prints for block

7 fat eighths of assorted red prints for block and flying-geese units

6 fat eighths of assorted gold prints for block and flying-geese units

⅓ yard *total* of assorted light prints for flying-geese units

⅛ yard of medium brown print for inner border

⅓ yard of red floral for outer border

¼ yard of brown tone on tone for binding

¾ yard of fabric for backing

27" × 27" piece of batting

Cutting

All measurements include ¼" seam allowances.

From *each* of 2 light prints for block, cut:
4 squares, 3" × 3" (8 total)

From *each* of 2 light prints for block, cut:
8 squares, 2" × 2" (16 total)

From *each* of 2 light prints for block, cut:
2 squares, 4½" × 4½" (4 total)

From *each* green print, cut:
2 squares, 3" × 3" (8 total)
1 square, 2" × 2" (4 total)

From *each* dark brown print, cut:
4 squares, 2" × 2" (8 total)

From *each* of 2 red prints, cut:
2 rectangles, 2" × 3½" (4 total)

From *each* of 4 gold prints, cut:
1 square, 4½" × 4½" (4 total)

From 1 gold print, cut:
1 square, 3½" × 3½"

From the remaining red and gold prints, cut a *total* of:
64 rectangles, 1½" × 2½"

From the light prints for flying geese, cut a *total* of:
128 squares, 1½" × 1½"

From the medium brown print, cut:
2 strips, 1½" × 42"; crosscut into:
    2 strips, 1½" × 14½"
    2 strips, 1½" × 12½"

From the red floral, cut:
3 strips, 2½" × 42"; crosscut into:
    2 strips, 2½" × 22½"
    2 strips, 2½" × 18½"

From the brown tone on tone, cut:
3 strips, 2¼" × 42"

Making the Center Block

Press all seam allowances in the direction indicated by the arrows.

1 Draw a diagonal line from corner to corner on the wrong side of the light 3" squares. Layer a marked square on a green 3" square, right sides together. Sew ¼" from both sides of the drawn line. Cut the unit apart on the marked line to make two half-square-triangle units. Trim the units to measure 2" square, including seam allowances. Make 16 units.

2 Lay out two different dark brown 2" squares, one green 2" square, two matching light 2" squares, and two sets of two matching half-square-triangle units. Make sure to place matching units diagonally across from each other. Sew the pieces together into rows. Join the rows to make a corner unit measuring 5" square, including seam allowances. Make four units.

Make 16 units.

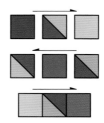

Make 4 units, 5" × 5".

3 Draw a diagonal line from corner to corner on the wrong side of the eight remaining light 2" squares. Place a marked square on one end of a red 2" × 3½" rectangle, right sides together. Sew on the marked line. Trim the excess corner fabric ¼" from the stitched line. Place a marked square on the opposite end of the red rectangle. Sew and trim as before to make a flying-geese unit that measures 2" × 3½", including seam allowances. Make four units.

Make 4 units,
2" × 3½".

4 Draw a diagonal line from corner to corner on the wrong side of the light 4½" squares. Repeat step 1, using the marked squares and the gold 4½" squares to make eight half-square-triangle units. Place two units with the same gold print right sides together, making sure that contrasting fabrics are facing each other. On the wrong side of the top unit, draw a diagonal line from corner to corner. Sew ¼" from both sides of the drawn line. Cut the unit apart on the marked line to make two hourglass units. Trim the units to measure 3½" square, including seam allowances. Repeat to make a total of eight units (one of each color combination will be extra).

3½"

3½"

Make 8 units.

5 Sew a flying-geese unit to an hourglass unit to make a side unit measuring 3½" × 5", including seam allowances. Make four units.

Make 4 units,
3½" × 5".

6 Lay out the corner units, side units, and gold 3½" square in rows, rotating the side and corner units as shown. Sew the units and square together into rows. Join the rows to make a block measuring 12½" square, including seam allowances.

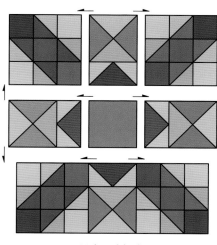

Make 1 block,
12½" × 12½".

4 Sew the 14½"-long flying-geese borders to the top and bottom of the quilt top as shown in the quilt assembly diagram below. Sew the 18½"-long borders to opposite sides of the quilt top. The quilt top should measure 18½" square, including seam allowances.

5 Sew the red floral 18½"-long strips to the top and bottom of the quilt top. Sew the red floral 22½"-long strips to opposite sides of the quilt top. The quilt top should measure 22½" square.

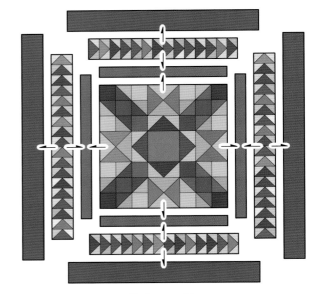

Quilt assembly

Making the Flying–Geese Border

1 Using two light 1½" squares and a red or gold 1½" × 2½" rectangle, repeat step 3 of "Making the Center Block" on page 25 to make a flying-geese unit measuring 1½" × 2½", including seam allowances. Make 64 units.

2 Join 14 units to make a border strip measuring 2½" × 14½", including seam allowances. Make two strips for the top and bottom borders. Join 18 units to make a border strip measuring 2½" × 18½", including seam allowances. Make two for the side borders.

Make 2 top/bottom borders,
2½" × 14½".

Make 2 side borders,
2½" × 18½".

3 Sew the medium brown 12½"-long strips to the top and bottom of the center block. Sew the medium brown 14½"-long strips to opposite sides of the block. The quilt top should measure 14½" square, including seam allowances.

Finishing the Quilt

For more details on the following finishing steps, visit ShopMartingale.com/HowtoQuilt for free downloadable information.

1 Layer the quilt top with batting and backing; baste the layers together.

2 Quilt by hand or machine. The quilt shown is machine quilted in the ditch, and a pumpkin seed design is quilted in the center block. A straight line is quilted throughout the flying-geese border, and the outer border features a feather motif.

3 Using the brown tone-on-tone 2¼"-wide strips, make binding and then attach the binding to the quilt.

Grandmother's Pride

My grandmother took pride in her handwork,
perfecting every stitch. I made this quilt in her memory.

FINISHED QUILT: 68¾" × 68¾" ◆ **FINISHED BLOCK:** 6¼" × 6¼"

Materials

Yardage is based on 42"-wide fabric.

1¼ yards *total* of assorted light prints for blocks

⅞ yard *total* of assorted medium to dark brown prints
    for blocks and leaves (collectively referred to as
    "medium brown")

⅝ yard *total* of assorted tan prints for blocks

¾ yard *total* of assorted red prints for blocks and berries

¼ yard *total* of assorted yellow and gold prints for blocks
    (collectively referred to as "gold")

1⅔ yards of dark brown print for setting squares

⅜ yard of red tone on tone for inner border

2⅛ yards of taupe print for outer border

⅛ yard of yellow print for flowerpots

¼ yard of chocolate brown print for appliqué stems

⅝ yard of dark red print for binding

4¼ yards of fabric for backing

75" × 75" piece of batting

Freezer paper

¼" bias-tape maker

Cutting

All measurements include ¼" seam allowances.

From the light prints, cut a *total* of:
82 squares, 3⅜" × 3⅜"; cut the squares into quarters
    diagonally to yield 328 side triangles
82 squares, 2" × 2"; cut the squares in half diagonally
    to yield 164 corner triangles

From the medium brown prints, cut a *total* of:
168 squares, 2" × 2"

From the tan prints, cut a *total* of:
164 squares, 2" × 2"

Continued on page 29

27

Continued from page 27

From the red prints, cut a *total* of:
164 squares, 2" × 2"

From the gold prints, cut a *total* of:
41 squares, 2" × 2"

From the dark brown print, cut:
8 strips, 6¾" × 42"; crosscut into 40 squares, 6¾" × 6¾"

From the red tone on tone, cut:
6 strips, 2" × 42"

From the taupe print, cut on the *lengthwise* grain:
2 strips, 5" × 68¾"
2 strips, 5" × 59¾"

From the chocolate brown print, cut on the *bias*:
8 strips, ½" × 12"

From the dark red print, cut:
8 strips, 2¼" × 42"

Making the Blocks

Press all seam allowances in the direction indicated by the arrows.

Lay out four medium brown squares, four tan squares, four red squares, one gold square, and eight light side triangles in five diagonal rows. Sew the squares and triangles together in rows. Join the rows and add the light corner triangles to make a block. Trim the block to measure 6¾" square, including seam allowances. Make 41 blocks.

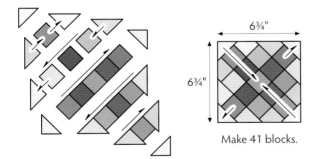

6¾"

6¾"

Make 41 blocks.

Assembling the Quilt Top

1   Lay out the blocks and dark brown squares in nine rows, alternating the blocks and squares in each row and from row to row as shown in the quilt assembly diagram below. Sew the blocks and squares together in rows. Join the rows to make the quilt-top center. The quilt top should measure 56¾" square, including seam allowances.

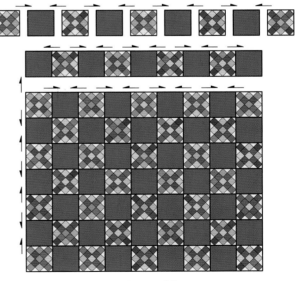

Quilt assembly

2 Join the red tone-on-tone strips end to end. From the pieced strips, cut four 56¾"-long strips. Sew two strips to opposite sides of the quilt top. Sew a medium brown square to each end of the remaining two strips. Sew these strips to the top and bottom of the quilt top. The quilt top should measure 59¾" square, including seam allowances.

3 Sew the taupe 59¾"-long strips to opposite sides of the quilt top. Sew the taupe 68¾"-long strips to the top and bottom of the quilt top. The quilt top should measure 68¾" square.

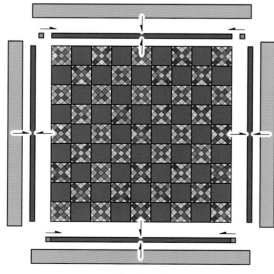

Adding borders

Choosing Fabrics

For each color, select fabrics that match in tone or depth of color. Within each color, use a variety of prints to add visual interest.

Adding the Appliqués

1 Using the patterns at right and referring to "Method 1: Freezer Paper" on page 72, prepare four yellow flowerpots, 24 red berries, and 32 medium brown leaves.

2 Referring to "Preparing Stems and Vines" on page 75, use the bias-tape maker and the chocolate brown strips to prepare eight ¼" × 12" vines.

3 Position a flowerpot in each corner of the taupe border. Tuck one end of a vine under the flowerpot, and arrange it in gentle curves. Add four leaves with the leaves overlapping the vines slightly. In the same way, place a second vine on the other side of the flowerpot. Add six berries. Stitch the appliqués in place, referring to "Stitching the Appliqués" on page 78.

Appliqué placement

Finishing the Quilt

For more details on the following finishing steps, visit ShopMartingale.com/HowtoQuilt for free downloadable information.

1 Layer the quilt top with batting and backing; baste the layers together.

2 Quilt by hand or machine. The quilt shown is machine quilted in the ditch along the seamlines and around the appliqué shapes. Curved triangles are quilted in the blocks, and the setting squares each feature a feathered wreath. A pumpkin seed design is quilted in the inner border and a feather design is used in the outer border.

3 Using the dark red 2¼"-wide strips, make binding and then attach the binding to the quilt.

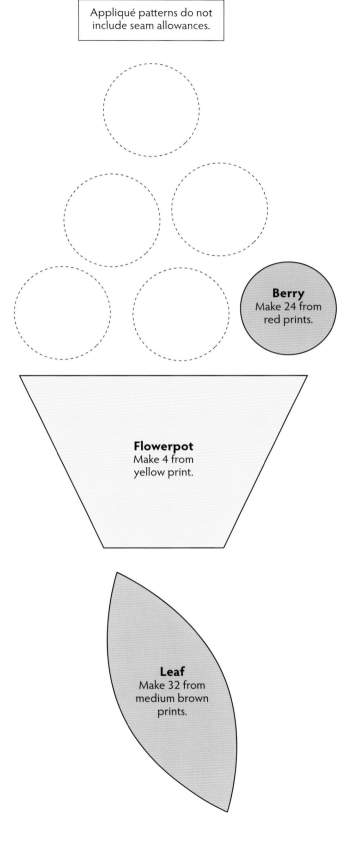

Appliqué patterns do not include seam allowances.

Berry
Make 24 from red prints.

Flowerpot
Make 4 from yellow print.

Leaf
Make 32 from medium brown prints.

Itty Bitty Roses

Seeing one fabric against another and enjoying how the combinations come alive always make me smile. Mini appliquéd roses and beautiful prints from the scrap bin make this a delightful little quilt to place in your home.

FINISHED QUILT: 11¾" × 11¾" ◆ **FINISHED BLOCK:** 2¼" × 2¼"

Materials

Yardage is based on 42"-wide fabric. Fat eighths measure 9" × 21". Fat quarters measure 18" × 21".

9 squares, 3" × 3" *each*, of assorted light prints for block backgrounds

Assorted scraps of light and dark prints for flower appliqués

2¾" × 7¼" rectangle *each* of 1 tan, 1 medium brown, and 1 dark brown print for border

2¾" × 11¾" rectangle of red floral for border

2¾" × 2¾" square *each* of 1 tan and 1 gold print for border corners

1 fat eighth of red check for binding

1 fat quarter of fabric for backing

16" × 16" piece of batting

Freezer paper or wash-away appliqué paper

Cutting

All measurements include ¼" seam allowances.

From the red check, cut:
3 strips, 2¼" × 21"

Appliquéing the Blocks

1 Using the patterns on page 34 and referring to "Method 1: Freezer Paper" on page 72 or "Method 2: Wash-Away Appliqué Paper" on page 75, prepare nine each of the center, ring 1, ring 2, and outer petals using the light and dark scraps.

2 Position a flower in the center of each light 3" square. Stitch the appliqués in place, referring to "Stitching the Appliqués" on page 78. Trim the blocks to measure 2¾" square, keeping the design centered.

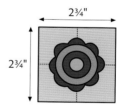

Appliqué placement

Use Scraps

Each rose is different. You only need a small piece of each print, making this a perfect quilt to use up your scraps. Mix it up, play with fabric combinations, put together fabrics that you love, and see what happens. Let the fun begin!

Assembling the Quilt Top

Press all seam allowances in the direction indicated by the arrows.

1 Lay out the blocks in three rows of three blocks each. Sew the blocks together into rows. Join the rows to make the quilt-top center, which should measure 7¼" square, including seam allowances.

2 Sew the tan rectangle to the left side of the quilt center. Sew the medium brown rectangle to the right side of the quilt center.

3 Sew the red floral rectangle to the top of the quilt. Join the gold and tan squares to the ends of the dark brown rectangle, and sew this strip to the bottom of the quilt. The quilt top should measure 11¾" square.

Finishing the Quilt

For more details on the following finishing steps, visit ShopMartingale.com/HowtoQuilt for free downloadable information.

1 Layer the quilt top with batting and backing; baste the layers together.

2 Quilt by hand or machine. The quilt shown is machine quilted in the ditch along the seamlines and around the appliqué shapes. The border is quilted with a free-motion feather design and the border corners are quilted with circles.

3 Using the red check 2¼"-wide strips, make binding and then attach the binding to the quilt.

Appliqué patterns do not include seam allowances.

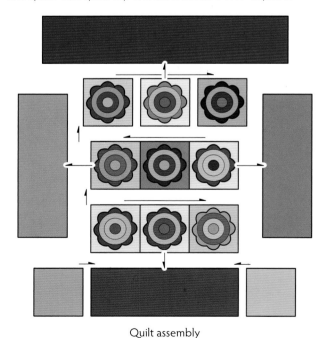

Quilt assembly

Ring 1
Make 9 from light and dark scraps.

Ring 2
Make 9 from light and dark scraps.

Center
Make 9 from light and dark scraps.

Outer petals
Make 9 from light and dark scraps.

Ring a Rosie

A sweet little quilt featuring pretty flowers made from specially selected fabric scraps, Ring a Rosie will brighten any table, cabinet, or wall. Sometimes it's the small things that bring the most joy.

FINISHED QUILT: 30½" × 30½" ◆ **FINISHED BLOCKS:** 8" × 8", 6" × 8", AND 6" × 6"

Materials

Yardage is based on 42"-wide fabric. Fat eighths measure 9" × 21". Fat quarters measure 18" × 21".

1 fat quarter *total* of assorted dark gold prints for blocks and inner-border corners

1 fat eighth *total* of assorted pink prints for blocks

1 fat eighth *total* of assorted blue prints for blocks

1 fat eighth *total* of assorted purple prints for blocks

1 fat eighth *total* of assorted yellow prints for blocks

½ yard *total* of assorted cream prints for blocks

1 fat eighth of medium brown print for stems

1 fat eighth of dark brown print for blocks

2 rectangles, 8" × 10" *each,* of different green prints for calyxes

2 rectangles, 5" × 7" *each,* of different brown prints for flowers

6" × 6" square of yellow print for flower centers

5 fat eighths of assorted light gold prints for inner border and outer-border corners

⅝ yard of brown floral for outer border

⅓ yard of gold tone on tone for binding

1 yard of fabric for backing

35" × 35" piece of batting

Freezer paper

¼" bias-tape maker

Cutting

All measurements include ¼" seam allowances.

From the dark gold prints, cut a *total* of:
8 squares, 3" × 3"
44 squares, 1½" × 1½"

From the pink prints, cut a *total* of:
2 squares, 3" × 3"
8 squares, 1½" × 1½"

From the blue prints, cut a *total* of:
2 squares, 3" × 3"
8 squares, 1½" × 1½"

From the purple prints, cut a *total* of:
2 squares, 3" × 3"
8 squares, 1½" × 1½"

From the yellow prints, cut a *total* of:
2 squares, 3" × 3"
8 squares, 1½" × 1½"

From the cream prints, cut a *total* of:
32 rectangles, 1½" × 4½"
16 squares, 3" × 3"
8 squares, 1½" × 1½"

From the medium brown print, cut on the *bias:*
8 strips, ½" × 5"

From the dark brown print, cut:
8 rectangles, 2½" × 4½"

Continued on page 37

Continued from page 35

From 1 light gold print, cut:

1 strip, 1½" × 20½"

2 squares, 5¼" × 5¼"; cut the squares into quarters diagonally to yield 8 triangles

From 1 light gold print, cut:

1 strip, 1½" × 20½"

1 square, 5¼" × 5¼"; cut the square into quarters diagonally to yield 4 triangles

From *each* of 2 light gold prints, cut:

1 strip, 1½" × 20½" (2 total)

From the remaining light gold print, cut:

1 square, 5¼" × 5¼"; cut the square into quarters diagonally to yield 4 triangles

From the brown floral, cut:

4 strips, 4½" × 22½"

From the gold tone on tone, cut:

4 strips, 2¼" × 42"

Making the Center Block

Press all seam allowances in the direction indicated by the arrows.

1 Sew two pink and two dark gold 1½" squares together to make a four-patch unit measuring 2½" square, including seam allowances. Make four units.

Make 4 units,
2½" × 2½".

2 Repeat step 1 using two dark gold and blue, purple, yellow, and cream 1½" squares instead of pink squares to make four units of each color combination. You'll have four dark gold squares left over for the inner-border corners.

Make 4 of each unit,
2½" × 2½".

3 Draw a diagonal line from corner to corner on the wrong side of the cream 3" squares. Layer a marked square on a dark gold 3" square, right sides together. Sew ¼" from both sides of the drawn line. Cut the unit apart on the marked line to make two half-square-triangle units. Trim the units to measure 2½" square, including seam allowances. Make 16 units. Set the units aside for step 2 of "Making the Side Blocks."

Make 16 units.

4 Repeat step 3 using two marked cream squares and pink, blue, purple, and yellow 3" squares instead of dark gold squares to make four units of each color combination.

Make 4 of each unit,
2½" × 2½".

5 Join two purple/gold four-patch units and two matching yellow half-square-triangle units to make a block unit measuring 4½" square. Make two units.

Make 2 units,
4½" × 4½".

6 Repeat step 5 using the remaining four-patch units and the purple, blue, and pink half-square-triangle units to make two block units of each color combination.

Make 2 of each unit,
4½" × 4½".

7 Lay out one unit of each color combination, rotating the units as shown. Sew the units together in rows. Join the rows to make the center block, which should measure 8½" square, including seam allowances.

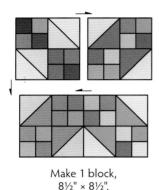

Make 1 block,
8½" × 8½".

Making the Side Blocks

1 Join eight cream 1½" × 4½" rectangles along their long edges to make a strip unit measuring 4½" × 8½", including seam allowances. Make four units.

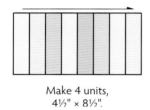

Make 4 units,
4½" × 8½".

2 Sew four dark gold/cream half-square-triangle units together as shown. Sew the triangle unit to the top of a strip unit to make a side block measuring 6½" × 8½", including seam allowances. Make four blocks.

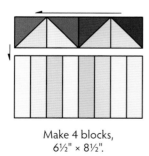

Make 4 blocks,
6½" × 8½".

3 Using the patterns on page 39 and referring to "Method 1: Freezer Paper" on page 72, prepare eight brown flowers, eight yellow flower centers, and eight green calyxes.

4 Referring to "Preparing Stems and Vines" on page 75, use the bias-tape maker and the medium brown strips to prepare eight ¼" × 5" stems.

5 Referring to the appliqué placement diagram, position two stems on each side block. Position a calyx on one end of each stem, tucking the stem under the calyx. Tuck a flower and flower center under each calyx. Stitch the appliqués in place, referring to "Stitching the Appliqués" on page 78.

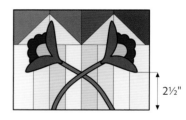

2½"

Appliqué placement

Making the Corner Blocks

Lay out one of the remaining blocks, one dark gold/cream four-patch unit, and two dark brown rectangles as shown. Sew the pieces together into rows. Join the rows to make a block measuring 6½" square, including seam allowances. Make four blocks.

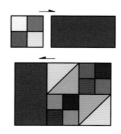

Make 4 blocks,
6½" × 6½".

Assembling the Quilt Top

1 Lay out the corner, side, and center blocks in three rows, rotating them as shown. Sew the blocks together into rows. Join the rows to make the quilt-top center, which should measure 20½" square, including seam allowances.

Quilt assembly

2 Sew light gold 1½" × 20½" strips to opposite sides of the quilt top. Sew a dark gold 1½" square to each end of the remaining two light gold strips. Sew the strips to the top and bottom. The quilt top should measure 22½" square, including seam allowances.

3 Sew two matching and two different light gold triangles together as shown to make a corner block measuring 4½" square, including seam allowances. The matching triangles should be opposite one another.

Make 4 blocks,
4½" × 4½".

4 Sew brown floral strips to opposite sides of the quilt top. Sew a corner block to each end of the remaining two brown floral strips. Sew the strips to the

top and bottom of the quilt top. The quilt top should measure 30½" square.

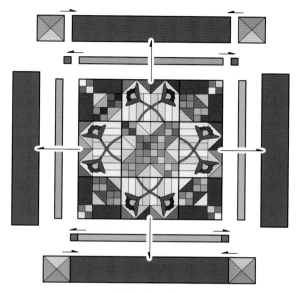

Adding borders

Finishing the Quilt

Visit ShopMartingale.com/HowtoQuilt for help with the following steps.

1 Layer the quilt top with batting and backing; baste together. Quilt by hand or machine. The quilt shown is machine quilted in the ditch along the seamlines and around the appliqués. A curved line is quilted in the triangles, and the outer border features a diagonal grid.

2 Using the gold tone-on-tone 2¼"-wide strips, make binding and then attach the binding to the quilt.

Appliqué patterns do not include seam allowances.

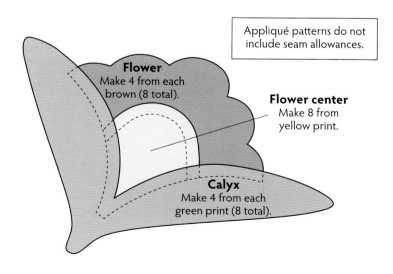

Flower
Make 4 from each brown (8 total).

Flower center
Make 8 from yellow print.

Calyx
Make 4 from each green print (8 total).

Simply Baskets

*Patchwork baskets, rambling vines, and pretty flowers set the scene for romance.
I have a love of Basket blocks, and mixing them with appliqué is absolute bliss.*

FINISHED QUILT: 57" × 56" ◆ **FINISHED BLOCK:** 6" × 6"

Materials

Yardage is based on 42"-wide fabric.

1 yard *total* of assorted light prints for blocks

⅜ yard *each* of assorted brown and yellow prints for
blocks and flower appliqués

½ yard *each* of assorted blue and pink prints for blocks
and flower appliqués

⅞ yard *total* of assorted plum prints for blocks and leaves

⅞ yard of gold print for sashing and inner border

¼ yard of dark purple print for sashing corners

1¾ yards of cream floral for setting triangles and
outer border

½ yard of yellow floral for leaves and vine

½ yard of gold tone on tone for binding

3½ yards of fabric for backing

62" × 63" piece of batting

Freezer paper

¼" bias-tape maker

Cutting

All measurements include ¼" seam allowances.

From the light prints, cut a *total* of:
13 squares, 3⅞" × 3⅞"; cut the squares in half diagonally
to yield 26 triangles (1 is extra)
63 squares, 2⅜" × 2⅜"; cut the squares in half diagonally
to yield 126 triangles (1 is extra)
25 sets of 2 matching rectangles, 2" × 3½" (50 total)

From the brown prints, cut a *total* of:
3 squares, 3⅞" × 3⅞"; cut the squares in half diagonally
to yield 6 triangles
15 squares, 2⅜" × 2⅜"; cut the squares in half diagonally
to yield 30 triangles

From the yellow prints, cut a *total* of:
3 squares, 3⅞" × 3⅞"; cut the squares in half diagonally
to yield 6 triangles
15 squares, 2⅜" × 2⅜"; cut the squares in half diagonally
to yield 30 triangles

From the blue prints, cut a *total* of:
3 squares, 3⅞" × 3⅞"; cut the squares in half diagonally
to yield 6 triangles
15 squares, 2⅜" × 2⅜"; cut the squares in half diagonally
to yield 30 triangles

From the pink prints, cut a *total* of:
4 squares, 3⅞" × 3⅞"; cut the squares in half diagonally
to yield 8 triangles (1 is extra)
18 squares, 2⅜" × 2⅜"; cut the squares in half diagonally
to yield 36 triangles (1 is extra)

From the plum prints, cut a *total* of:
13 squares, 3⅞" × 3⅞"; cut the squares in half diagonally
to yield 26 triangles (1 is extra)
25 squares, 2⅜" × 2⅜"; cut the squares in half diagonally
to yield 50 triangles

From the gold print, cut:
14 strips, 2" × 42"; crosscut *11 of the strips* into 64
rectangles, 2" × 6½"

From the dark purple print, cut:
40 squares, 2" × 2"

Continued on page 42

Continued from page 41

From the cream floral, cut on the *lengthwise* grain:

2 strips, 6½" × 56"

2 strips, 4½" × 45"

3 squares, 11⅞" × 11⅞"; cut the squares into quarters diagonally to yield 12 side triangles

2 squares, 7¼" × 7¼"; cut the squares in half diagonally to yield 4 corner triangles

From the yellow floral, cut on the *bias* and piece as necessary to make:

4 strips, ½" × 32"

4 strips, ½" × 7"

From the gold tone on tone, cut:

7 strips, 2¼" × 42"

Making the Blocks

Press all seam allowances in the direction indicated by the arrows.

1 Sew a light 2⅜" triangle to a brown 2⅜" triangle to make a half-square-triangle unit measuring 2" square, including seam allowances. Make 30 units. Repeat using the blue, yellow, and pink 2⅜" triangles in place of the brown triangles to make the number of units indicated of each color combination.

Make 30 of each unit, 2" × 2". Make 35 units, 2" × 2".

2 Sew a plum 3⅞" triangle to a brown 3⅞" triangle to make a half-square-triangle unit measuring 3½" square, including seam allowances. Make six units. Repeat using the blue, yellow, and pink 3⅞" triangles in place of the brown triangles to make the number of units indicated of each color combination.

Make 6 of each unit, 3½" × 3½".

Make 7 units, 3½" × 3½".

3 Lay out five brown/light 2" half-square-triangle units and one brown/plum 3½" half-square-triangle unit as shown. Sew the units together to make a basket unit measuring 5" square, including seam allowances.

Make 1 unit, 5" × 5".

4 Sew a plum 2⅜" triangle to one end of a light rectangle to make a side unit. Use a matching light rectangle to make a mirror-image side unit.

Make 1 of each unit.

5 Lay out the basket unit, the side units from step 4, and a light 3⅞" triangle as shown. Sew the side units to the basket unit; add the light triangle to make a block measuring 6½" square, including seam allowances. Make six brown blocks.

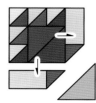

Make 6 blocks, 6½" × 6½".

6 Repeat steps 3–5 to make six blue, six yellow, and seven pink blocks.

Make 6 of each block, 6½" × 6½".

Make 7 blocks, 6½" × 6½".

Assembling the Quilt Top

1 Lay out the blocks, gold rectangles, dark purple squares, and cream floral side and corner triangles in diagonal rows as shown. Sew the pieces together in rows. Join the rows, adding the corner triangles last. Trim and square up the quilt top, making sure to leave ¼" beyond the points of all sashing squares for seam allowances. The quilt-top center should measure 45" square, including seam allowances.

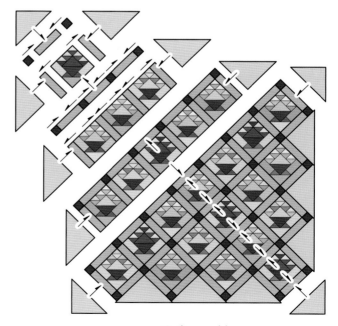

Quilt assembly

2 Join the remaining gold print 2"-wide strips end to end. From the pieced strip, cut two 45"-long strips. Join a gold strip and a cream floral 45"-long strip along their long edges to make a 6" × 45" border strip. Sew the strips to the top and bottom of the quilt top. Sew the cream floral 6½"-wide strips to opposite sides of the quilt top. The quilt top should measure 57" × 56".

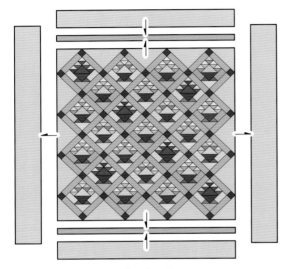

Adding borders

Adding the Appliqués

1 Using the patterns on page 45 and referring to "Method 1: Freezer Paper" on page 72, prepare the following shapes from the fabrics indicated.

- Pink print: two roses, four flower centers D, and four flower centers E

- Brown print: two flower centers A, four flower centers D, and four calyxes

- Blue print: two flower centers B, four half roses, four calyxes, and 18 berries

- Yellow print: two flower centers C, four half roses, and four flower centers E

- Plum prints: 44 large leaves

- Yellow floral: 16 small leaves

2 Referring to "Preparing Stems and Vines" on page 75, use the bias-tape maker and the yellow floral strips to prepare four ¼" × 32" vines and four ¼" × 7" vines.

3 Refer to "Building Appliqué Units" on page 78 to construct the rose and half rose motifs.

4 Refer to the photo on page 42 and the appliqué placement diagram below as needed. On the left and right sides, position a rose in the center of the outer border, placing it on top of the setting triangle. Place a 32"-long vine on each side of the rose, tucking one end of each vine under the rose and curving the vine around the corner. Position a half rose and 7"-long vine on each side of the center rose, tucking the ends of the vines under the long vine and calyx. Place three berries along the end of each vine and three berries on the outer edge of the center rose. Position the leaves along the vine, overlapping the vines slightly. Stitch the appliqués in place, referring to "Stitching the Appliqués" on page 78.

Appliqué placement

Finishing the Quilt

For more details on the following finishing steps, visit ShopMartingale.com/HowtoQuilt for free downloadable information.

1 Layer the quilt top with batting and backing; baste the layers together.

2 Quilt by hand or machine. The quilt shown is machine quilted in the ditch along the seamlines and around the appliqués. The basket blocks are quilted with a curved design. Straight lines are quilted throughout the sashing and gold border, and the outer border features a free-motion feather motif.

3 Using the gold tone-on-tone 2¼"-wide strips, make binding and then attach the binding to the quilt.

Appliqué patterns do not include seam allowances.

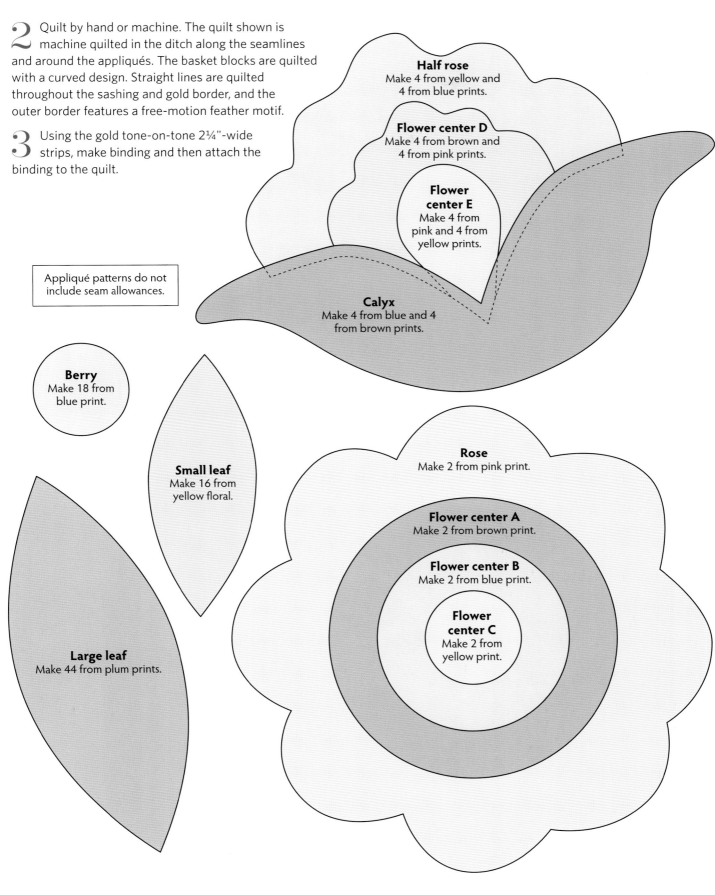

Half rose
Make 4 from yellow and 4 from blue prints.

Flower center D
Make 4 from brown and 4 from pink prints.

Flower center E
Make 4 from pink and 4 from yellow prints.

Calyx
Make 4 from blue and 4 from brown prints.

Berry
Make 18 from blue print.

Small leaf
Make 16 from yellow floral.

Large leaf
Make 44 from plum prints.

Rose
Make 2 from pink print.

Flower center A
Make 2 from brown print.

Flower center B
Make 2 from blue print.

Flower center C
Make 2 from yellow print.

Goose Crossing

Flying Geese blocks are brought to life with buried treasures from the scrap bin. Bold appliquéd blooms add to the mix and enhance the design. Goose Crossing is truly a quilt to be desired.

FINISHED QUILT: 74½" × 74½" ◆ **FINISHED BLOCK:** 20" × 20"

Materials

Yardage is based on 42"-wide fabric.

6¾ yards *total* of assorted light prints for blocks and outer border

½ yard *total* of assorted red prints for blocks and flowers

1½ yards *total* of assorted medium and dark prints for blocks (collectively referred to as "dark")

⅞ yard *total* of assorted black prints for flowers

½ yard *total* of assorted purple prints for flowers

½ yard *total* of assorted gold prints for flowers

⅛ yard *total* of assorted yellow prints for flowers

1¼ yards *total* of assorted green prints for leaves

¼ yard of brown print for stems

⅓ yard of red floral for inner border

⅝ yard of red tone on tone for binding

6¾ yards of fabric for backing

81" × 81" piece of batting

Freezer paper

¼" bias-tape maker

Cutting

All measurements include ¼" seam allowances.

From the light prints, cut:
9 squares, 15½" × 15½"; cut the squares into quarters diagonally to yield 36 A triangles
8 rectangles, 6½" × 16½"
8 rectangles, 6½" × 10"
4 rectangles, 6½" × 11½"
4 squares, 6½" × 6½"
9 squares, 4½" × 4½"
18 squares, 3¾" × 3¾"; cut the squares in half diagonally to yield 36 B triangles
360 squares, 2½" × 2½"

From the red prints, cut:
36 rectangles, 2½" × 4½"

From the dark prints, cut:
144 rectangle, 2½" × 4½"

From the brown print, cut:
88 strips, ½" × 5"

From the red floral, cut:
7 strips, 1½" × 42"

From the red tone on tone, cut:
8 strips, 2¼" × 42"

Making the Blocks

Press all seam allowances in the direction indicated by the arrows.

1 Draw a diagonal line from corner to corner on the wrong side of the light 2½" squares. Place a marked square on one end of a red rectangle, right sides together. Sew on the marked line. Trim the excess corner fabric ¼" from the stitched line. Place a marked square on the opposite end of the red rectangle. Sew and trim as before to make a flying-geese unit that measures 2½" × 4½", including seam allowances. Make 36 red units.

Make 36 units,
2½" × 4½".

2 Repeat step 1 using the remaining marked squares and the dark rectangles to make 144 flying-geese units measuring 2½" × 4½", including seam allowances.

Make 144 units,
2½" × 4½".

3 Join one red unit, four dark units, and one light B triangle as shown to make a flying-geese strip. Make 36.

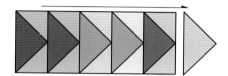

Make 36 strips.

4 Lay out four flying-geese strips, four light A triangles, and one light 4½" square as shown. Join the pieces in diagonal rows. Join the rows to make a block measuring 20½" square, including seam allowances. Make nine blocks.

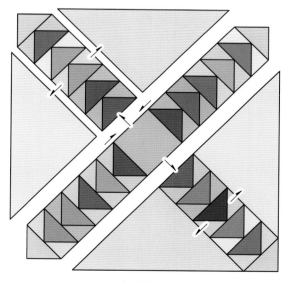

Make 9 blocks,
20½" × 20½".

Adding the Appliqués

1 Using the patterns on page 51 and referring to "Method 1: Freezer Paper" on page 72, prepare 52 black flowers, 25 purple flowers, 77 gold flower centers A, 52 yellow flower centers B, 25 red flower centers B, and 156 green leaves.

2 Referring to "Preparing Stems and Vines" on page 75, use the bias-tape maker and the brown strips to prepare 88 stems, ¼" × 5".

3 Refer to "Building Appliqué Units" on page 78 to assemble the flowers and flower centers.

4 Fold each block in half vertically and horizontally and lightly crease to create centering lines. Position a purple flower in the center of each block. Place a black flower on each A triangle, about ⅜" from the outer edge, centering the flower on the crease. Place a stem on each crease, tucking the ends under the flowers. Place two leaves on each stem, overlapping the stem slightly as shown in the appliqué placement diagram below. Stitch the appliqués in place, referring to "Stitching the Appliqués" on page 78. Set aside the remaining flowers, leaves, and stems for the outer border.

Appliqué placement

2 Join the red floral strips end to end. From the pieced strip, cut two 60½"-long strips and two 62½"-long strips. Sew the 60½"-long strips to opposite sides of the quilt top. Sew the 62½"-long strips to the top and bottom of the quilt top. The quilt top should measure 62½" square, including seam allowances.

3 Join two light 6½" × 16½" rectangles, one light 6½" × 11½" rectangle, and two light 6½" × 10" rectangles to make a border strip measuring 6½" × 62½", including seam allowances. Make two for the side borders. Make two more border strips in the same way, and add a light 6½" square to each end to make the top and bottom borders that measure 6½" × 74½", including seam allowances.

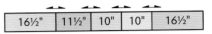

Make 2 side borders,
6½" × 62½".

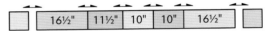

Make 2 top/bottom borders,
6½" × 74½".

Assembling the Quilt Top

1 Lay out the blocks in three rows of three blocks each. Sew the blocks together into rows. Join the rows to make the quilt-top center, which should measure 60½" square, including seam allowances.

4 Sew the borders to opposite sides of the quilt top and then to the top and bottom. The quilt top should now measure 74½" square.

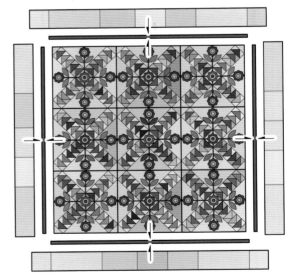

Adding borders

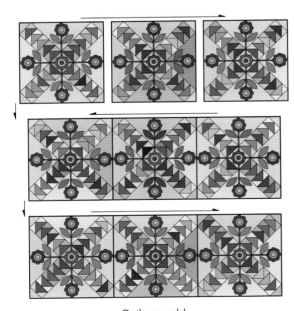

Quilt assembly

5 Referring to the photo on page 48 and the diagram below, appliqué three black flowers, four purple flowers, 19 leaves, and 12 stems on each outer border. Appliqué a black flower, two leaves, and one stem in each corner.

Finishing the Quilt

For more details on the following finishing steps, visit ShopMartingale.com/HowtoQuilt for free downloadable information.

1 Layer the quilt top with batting and backing; baste the layers together.

2 Quilt by hand or machine. The quilt shown is machine quilted in the ditch along the seamlines and around the appliqué shapes. Curved triangles are quilted in the flying-geese strips and a feather design is quilted in the background. An additional free-motion feather design is used in the border.

3 Using the red tone-on-tone 2¼"-wide strips, make binding and then attach the binding to the quilt.

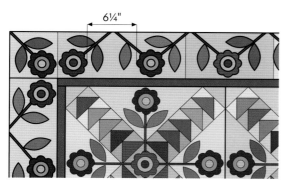

6¼"

Appliqué placement

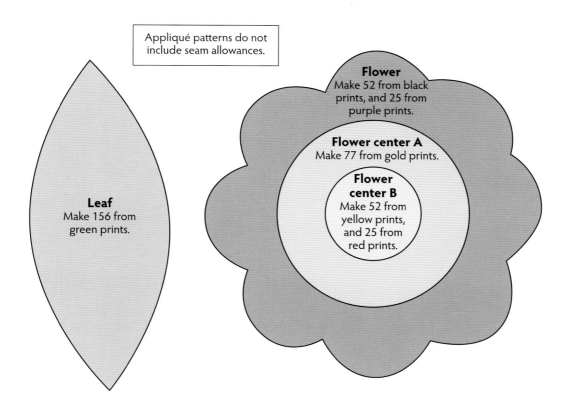

Appliqué patterns do not include seam allowances.

Leaf
Make 156 from green prints.

Flower
Make 52 from black prints, and 25 from purple prints.

Flower center A
Make 77 from gold prints.

Flower center B
Make 52 from yellow prints, and 25 from red prints.

Candy Baskets

I was intrigued by a picture of an antique quilt that used an unusual Basket block design I had never seen. Using a large selection of fabrics adds interest to the block, while the red-and-white striped handles remind me of candy canes.

FINISHED QUILT: 32½" × 32½" ◆ **FINISHED BLOCK:** 12" × 12"

Materials

Yardage is based on 42"-wide fabric. Fat eighths measure 9" × 21".

¼ yard of pink print A for blocks

1 fat eighth of red print for blocks

1 fat eighth *total* of assorted light prints for blocks

¼ yard *total* of assorted dark prints for blocks

¾ yard of red stripe for basket handles and binding

½ yard of pink dot for blocks

¼ yard of pink print B for blocks

⅝ yard of pink print C for border

1 fat eighth of pink print D for border corners

1⅛ yards of fabric for backing

37" × 37" piece of batting

Freezer paper

½" bias-tape maker

Cutting

All measurements include ¼" seam allowances.

From pink print A, cut:
2 strips, 2" × 42"; crosscut into 8 rectangles, 2" × 9"
2 squares, 3⅞" × 3⅞"; cut the squares in half diagonally to yield 4 triangles

From the red print, cut:
4 squares, 2" × 2"
4 squares, 2⅜" × 2⅜"; cut the squares in half diagonally to yield 8 triangles

From the light prints, cut a *total* of:
5 sets of 2 matching squares, 2⅜" × 2⅜" (10 total); cut the squares in half diagonally to yield 20 triangles

From the dark prints, cut a *total* of:
36 squares, 2" × 2"

From the red stripe, cut *on the bias*:
2¼"-wide strips, enough to yield 150"
4 strips, 1" × 15"

From the pink dot, cut:
2 squares, 11⅜" × 11⅜"; cut the squares in half diagonally to yield 4 triangles

From pink print B, cut:
3 strips, 2" × 42"; crosscut into:
   4 rectangles, 2" × 12½"
   4 rectangles, 2" × 11"

From pink print C, cut:
4 strips, 4½" × 24½"

From pink print D, cut:
4 squares, 4½" × 4½"

Making the Basket Blocks

Press all seam allowances in the direction indicated by the arrows.

1 Trace the trapezoid pattern on page 57 onto freezer paper. Cut out the freezer-paper template directly on the outer solid lines. Iron the template onto the right side of a pink A rectangle. Using scissors or a rotary cutter and ruler, cut out the fabric piece. Make a total of four trapezoids. Iron the freezer-paper template on the *wrong* side of each remaining pink A rectangle. Cut out the pieces to make four reversed trapezoids.

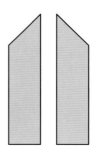

Make 4 of each unit.

2 Join red triangles to two adjacent edges of a red square. Sew the pieced triangle unit to the diagonal edge of a pink A triangle to make unit A, which should measure 3½" square, including seam allowances. Make four units.

Unit A.
Make 4 units,
3½" × 3½".

3 Join one light triangle and three dark squares to make a row. Sew a trapezoid to the bottom of the row to make unit B. Make four identical units.

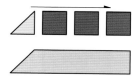
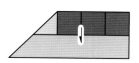

Unit B.
Make 4 units.

4 Join three light triangles and six dark squares in three rows. Join the rows and sew a light triangle to the top of the unit. Sew a reversed trapezoid to the pieced triangle to make unit C. Make four identical units.

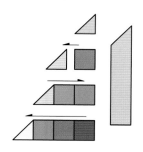
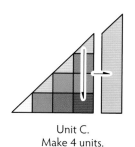

Unit C.
Make 4 units.

5 Sew an A unit to a B unit. Add a C unit to make a basket unit. Make four basket units.

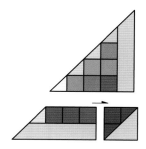
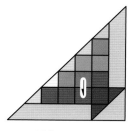

Make 4 units.

6 Referring to "Preparing Stems and Vines" on page 75, use the bias-tape maker and the red stripe strips to prepare four ½" × 15" handles.

7 Trace the basket handle guide on page 57 onto freezer paper and cut it out. Fold a pink dot triangle in half and lightly crease to mark the center of the long side. Iron the basket handle guide to the right side of a triangle, matching the centerline on the template with the creased line. Align a handle with the curved edge of the freezer-paper template; baste. Remove the freezer-paper template. Stitch the handle in place, referring to "Stitching the Appliqués" on page 78. Make four units.

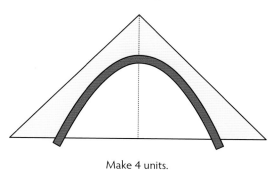

Make 4 units.

8 Sew a handle unit to a basket unit. Make four units that measure 11" square, including seam allowances.

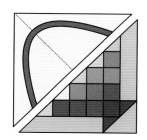
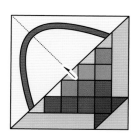

Make 4 units,
11" × 11".

9 Sew a 2" × 11" pink B rectangle to one side of the unit. Sew a 2" × 12½" pink B rectangle to an adjacent side of the unit to make a block measuring 12½" square, including seam allowances. Make four blocks.

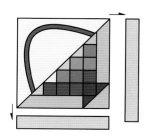
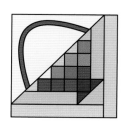

Make 4 blocks,
12½" × 12½".

Assembling the Quilt Top

1 Lay out the blocks in two rows of two blocks each, rotating them as shown in the quilt assembly diagram below. Sew the blocks together into rows. Join the rows to make the quilt-top center, which should measure 24½" square, including the seam allowances.

2 Sew pink C strips to opposite sides of the quilt top. Sew a pink D square to each end of the remaining pink C strips. Sew these strips to the top and bottom of the quilt top. The quilt top should measure 32½" square.

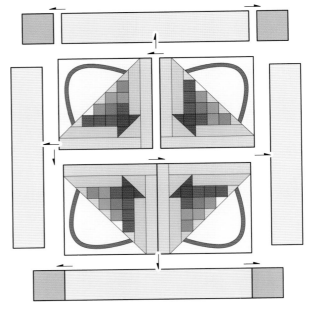

Quilt assembly

Finishing the Quilt

For more details on the following finishing steps, visit ShopMartingale.com/HowtoQuilt for free downloadable information.

1 Layer the quilt top with batting and backing; baste the layers together.

2 Quilt by hand or machine. The quilt shown is machine quilted in the ditch. Curved lines are quilted in the squares in the baskets, and a flower design is added between the handles and the baskets. The border features a free-motion feather motif.

3 Using the red stripe 2¼"-wide bias strips, make binding and then attach the binding to the quilt.

Autumn Bouquet

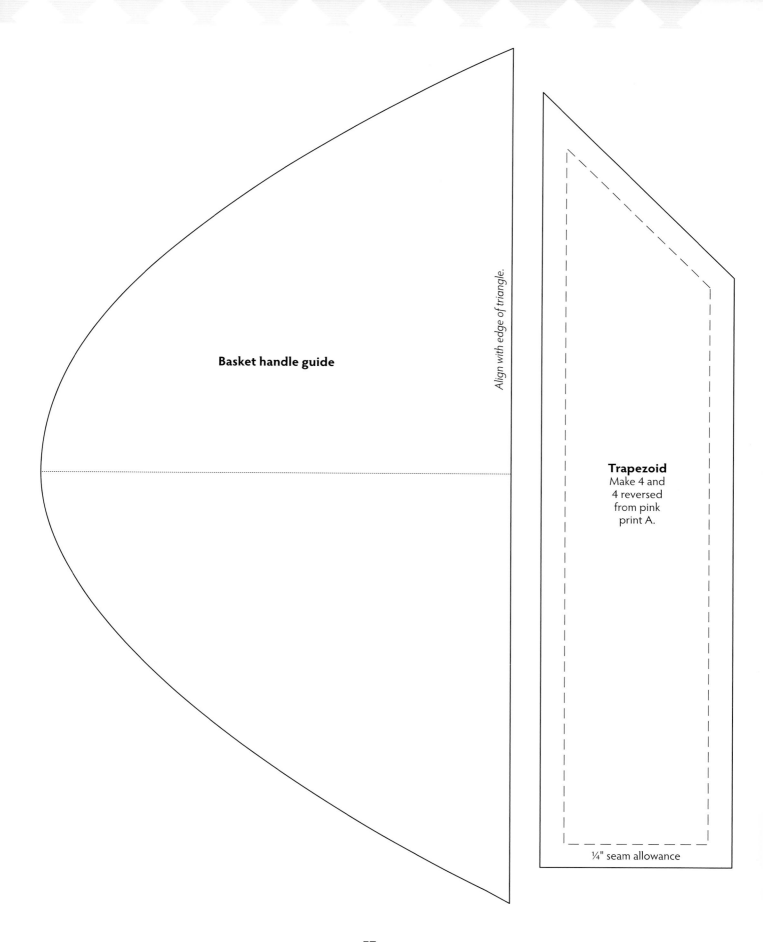

Basket handle guide

Align with edge of triangle.

Trapezoid
Make 4 and
4 reversed
from pink
print A.

¼" seam allowance

Purple Daisies

This petite patchwork quilt has just the right amount of appliqué for anyone new to the techniques. Daisies and vines softly frame the center patchwork block with a lovely mix of purples and golds.

FINISHED QUILT 28½" × 28½" ◆ **FINISHED CENTER BLOCK** 12" × 12"

Materials

Yardage is based on 42"-wide fabric. Fat quarters measure 18" × 21". Fat eighths measure 9" × 21".

⅞ yard of gold tone on tone for quilt center and borders

½ yard *total* of 5 assorted medium plum prints for quilt center and outer border

2 rectangles, 6" × 12" *each*, of different light gold prints for quilt center

2 squares, 5" × 5" *each*, of different dark gold prints for quilt center and flower centers

1 fat eighth of light green print for quilt center

2 fat eighths of different blue prints for quilt center

1 fat quarter of dark purple print for quilt center and petals

3 fat eighths of assorted green prints for leaves

1 fat eighth of brown print for stems

⅓ yard of gold stripe for binding

1 yard of fabric for backing

33" × 33" piece of batting

Freezer paper

¼" bias-tape maker

Cutting

All measurements include ¼" seam allowances.

From the gold tone on tone, cut:
2 strips, 4½" × 24½"
2 strips, 4½" × 16½"
4 squares, 2⅞" × 2⅞"
56 squares, 2½" × 2½"

From 1 medium plum print, cut:
16 rectangles, 2½" × 4½"

From *each* of 2 medium plum prints, cut:
2 squares, 2⅞" × 2⅞" (4 total)
4 rectangles, 2½" × 4½" (8 total)

From 1 medium plum print, cut:
8 rectangles, 2½" × 4½"

From the remaining medium plum print, cut:
4 squares, 2⅞" × 2⅞"; cut the squares in half diagonally to yield 8 triangles

From 1 light gold print, cut:
4 squares, 2⅞" × 2⅞"; cut the squares in half diagonally to yield 8 triangles

From the remaining light gold print, cut:
8 squares, 2½" × 2½"

From 1 dark gold print, cut:
1 square, 4⅞" × 4⅞"; cut the squares in half diagonally to yield 2 triangles

From the light green print, cut:
3 squares, 4⅞" × 4⅞"; cut the squares in half diagonally to yield 6 triangles

Continued on page 60

Continued from page 59

From 1 blue print, cut:
4 rectangles, 2½" × 4½"

From the other blue print, cut:
4 squares, 2½" × 2½"

From the dark purple print, cut:
4 rectangles, 2½" × 4½"

From the brown print, cut on the *bias:*
8 strips, ½" × 9½"

From the gold stripe, cut:
4 strips, 2¼" × 42"

Making the Center Unit

Press all seam allowances in the direction indicated by the arrows.

1 Draw a diagonal line from corner to corner on the wrong side of the gold tone-on-tone 2⅞" squares. Layer a marked square on a medium plum square, right sides together. Sew ¼" from both sides of the drawn line. Cut the unit apart on the marked line to make two

half-square-triangle units measuring 2½" square, including seam allowances. Make eight units.

Make 8 units,
2½" × 2½".

2 Sew light gold triangles to the two plum sides of a half-square-triangle unit. Make four units using the same medium plum print. Set aside the remaining four half-square-triangle units for the outer border.

Make 4 units.

3 Sew a pieced triangle unit to a dark gold triangle. Make two. Sew a pieced triangle unit to a light green triangle. Make two. The units should measure 4½" square, including seam allowances.

Make 2 of each unit,
4½" × 4½".

4 Arrange the units from step 3 in two rows, placing like colors in opposite corners. Sew the units together into rows. Join the rows to make the center unit, which should measure 8½" square, including seam allowances.

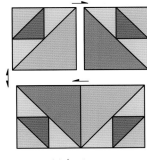

Make 1 unit,
8½" × 8½".

Making the Flying–Geese Units

1 Draw a diagonal line from corner to corner on the wrong side of the gold tone-on-tone 2½" squares. Place a marked square on one end of a blue rectangle, right sides together. Sew on the marked line. Trim the excess corner fabric, ¼" from the stitched line. Place a marked square on the opposite end of the blue rectangle. Sew and trim as before to make a flying-geese unit that measures 2½" × 4½", including seam allowances. Make four units.

Make 4 units,
2½" × 4½".

2 Set aside eight matching medium plum rectangles for the inner border. Repeat step 1 using the remaining marked gold squares and 24 of the medium plum rectangles to make 24 units. Draw a diagonal line from corner to corner on the wrong side of the light gold squares. Use the marked light gold squares and the dark purple rectangles to make four flying-geese units. Set aside the medium plum flying-geese units for the outer border.

Make 24 units,   Make 4 units,
2½" × 4½".   2½" × 4½".

3

Sew light green triangles to two opposite corners of the unit from step 2. Sew light green triangles to the remaining corners to complete the center block. The block should measure 12½" square, including seam allowances.

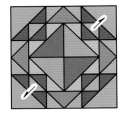
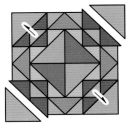

Make 1 block,
12½" × 12½".

4

Join two matching medium plum rectangles and one dark purple flying-geese unit to make a border strip measuring 2½" × 12½", including seam allowances. Make two for the top and bottom borders. Make two side borders in the same manner, adding a blue square to each end. The side borders should measure 2½" × 16½", including seam allowances.

Make 2 top/bottom borders,
2½" × 12½".

Make 2 side borders,
2½" × 16½".

Assembling the Quilt Center

1

Sew medium plum triangles to opposite ends of blue flying-geese units to make four side units.

Make 4 units.

2

Sew side units to opposite sides of the center unit, and then sew side units to the top and bottom of the unit.

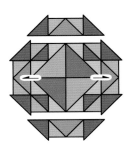

Make 1 unit.

5

Sew the borders to the top and bottom of the center block and then to each side. The quilt center should measure 16½" square, including seam allowances.

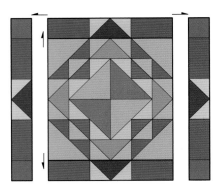

Make 1 quilt center,
16½" × 16½".

Autumn Bouquet

6 Sew the gold tone-on-tone 4½" × 16½" strips to the top and bottom of the quilt center. Sew the gold tone-on-tone 4½" × 24½" strips to opposite sides of the quilt center. The quilt top should measure 24½" square, including seam allowances.

Quilt assembly

Adding the Appliqués

1 Using the patterns on page 64 and referring to "Method 1: Freezer Paper" on page 72, prepare 32 dark purple petals, four dark gold flower centers, and 32 green leaves.

2 Referring to "Preparing Stems and Vines" on page 75, use the bias-tape maker and the brown strips to prepare eight ¼" × 9½" vines.

No Need to Wash

Preparing the appliqué shapes using method 1 (page 72) works well for borders because the quilt top can be fully assembled without needing to wash the border or the quilt top to remove the glue or starch.

3 Position eight petals in each corner of the gold border to make a daisy. Tuck one end of a vine under the daisy, and then position the leaves along the vine as shown in the appliqué placement diagram. Place a flower center in the middle of each daisy. Stitch the appliqués in place, referring to "Stitching the Appliqués" on page 78.

Appliqué placement

Adding the Outer Border

1 Join six medium purple flying-geese units to make a border strip measuring 2½" × 24½", including seam allowances. Make two for the side borders. Make two more strips in the same way, and add a half-square-triangle unit to each end to complete top and bottom borders measuring 2½" × 28½", including seam allowances.

Make 2 side borders, 2½" × 24½".

Make 2 top/bottom borders, 2½" × 28½".

2 Sew the borders to opposite sides of the quilt top and then to the top and bottom. The quilt top should now measure 28½" square.

Adding borders

Finishing the Quilt

For more details on the following finishing steps, visit ShopMartingale.com/HowtoQuilt for free downloadable information.

1 Layer the quilt top with batting and backing; baste the layers together.

2 Quilt by hand or machine. The quilt shown is machine quilted in the ditch and then quilted with curved lines in the quilt center. The appliqué border features a free-motion feather design and pebbles. The outer border is quilted with curved triangles.

3 Using the gold stripe 2¼"-wide strips, make binding and then attach the binding to the quilt.

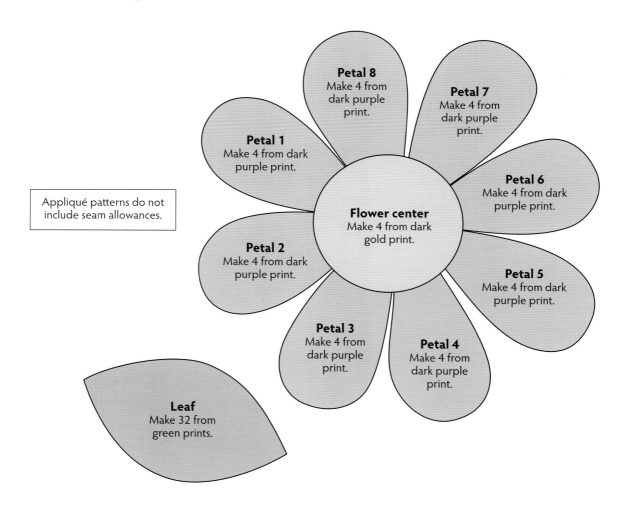

Appliqué patterns do not include seam allowances.

Petal 8
Make 4 from dark purple print.

Petal 7
Make 4 from dark purple print.

Petal 1
Make 4 from dark purple print.

Petal 6
Make 4 from dark purple print.

Flower center
Make 4 from dark gold print.

Petal 2
Make 4 from dark purple print.

Petal 5
Make 4 from dark purple print.

Petal 3
Make 4 from dark purple print.

Petal 4
Make 4 from dark purple print.

Leaf
Make 32 from green prints.

Sharon's Surprise

Antique quilts are always a wonderful source of inspiration. For Sharon's Surprise I played with color and used only hues I had seen in vintage appliqué quilts. It was such a surprise to see the effect created using colors from the past. Bringing pink and red together in the same quilt posed a learning curve for me.

FINISHED QUILT 30½" × 30½" ◆ **FINISHED CENTER BLOCK** 20" × 20"

3 fat eighths of assorted green prints for stems and leaves

3" × 3" square of brown print for center circle

⅓ yard of blue print for binding

1 yard of fabric for backing

35" × 35" piece of batting

Wash-away appliqué paper

¼" bias-tape maker

Materials

Yardage is based on 42"-wide fabric. Fat eighths measure 9" × 21".

⅞ yard of white solid for appliqué background and outer border

¾ yard *total* of 2 red prints for medallion circle, large center scallops, large corner flowers, and border scallops

⅜ yard of blue solid for small center scallops, flower centers, and inner border

½ yard of yellow print for medallion circle ovals, small corner flowers, and border scallop ovals

1 fat eighth of pink print for circle flowers and small flower centers

Cutting

All measurements include ¼" seam allowances.

From the white solid, cut:
1 strip, 22½" × 42"; crosscut into:
    4 strips, 4½" × 22½"
    1 square, 21½" × 21½"
4 squares, 4½" × 4½"

From the blue solid, cut:
2 strips, 1½" × 20½"
2 strips, 1½" × 22½"

From the yellow print, cut:
1 square, 8" × 8"
20 rectangles, 3" × 4"

From *1* green print, cut:
4 strips, ½" × 8"

From the blue print, cut:
4 strips, 2¼" × 42"

Appliquéing the Center Block

1 Using the patterns on pages 68–70 and referring to "Method 2: Wash-Away Appliqué Paper" on page 75, prepare the following for appliqué.

- Use one red print to prepare one medallion circle, eight large center scallops, and 10 border scallops.

- Use the second red print to prepare four large corner flowers and 10 border scallops.

- Use the blue solid to prepare eight small center scallops, four flower centers for the circle flowers, and four flower centers for the corner flowers.

- Use the yellow print to prepare four small corner flowers.

- Use the pink print to prepare four circle flowers and four small flower centers for the corner flowers.

- Use each green print to prepare eight leaves (24 total).

- Use the brown square to prepare one center circle.

2 Referring to "Preparing Stems and Vines" on page 75, use the bias-tape maker and the green strips to prepare four ¼" × 4" stems and four ¼" × 2" stems.

3 Refer to "Building Appliqué Units" on page 78 to construct the center scallops and corner flowers.

4 The small ovals in the medallion circle and border scallops are stitched using reverse appliqué. Cut out the center of the ovals, and then fold the edges over the appliqué paper. Place the prepared medallion circle on top of the yellow square. Both fabrics should have right sides facing up. Machine stitch around the edge of each oval. Trim the excess yellow print, leaving a ¼" seam allowance. In the same way, reverse appliqué a red border scallop on top of each yellow rectangle.

5 Fold the white 21½" square in half diagonally in both directions; finger-press to establish centering lines. Unfold, and fold in half vertically and horizontally; crease to create centering lines. Referring to the appliqué placement diagram, position a flower in each corner. Place a 4"-long stem on each diagonal crease, tucking one end under the flower. Position two leaves on each side of the stem. Position a circle flower, flower center, 2"-long stem, and two leaves on the horizontal and vertical creases. Place the appliquéd red circle in the center of the white square and the brown circle in the center of the red circle. Position the prepared center scallops around the circle, tucking the edge of each scallop under the medallion circle and on top of each stem. Stitch the appliqués in place, referring to "Stitching the Appliqués" on page 78.

6 Trim the appliquéd block to measure 20½" square, keeping the design centered.

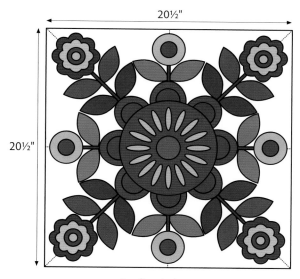

20½"

20½"

Appliqué placement

What is Reverse Appliqué?

The term "reverse appliqué" applies when the desired shape is cut out of the top layer of fabric and appliquéd along the inner edge of this opening to reveal the fabric below.

Assembling the Quilt Top

1. Sew the blue 20½"-long strips to opposite sides of the appliquéd block. Sew the blue 22½"-long strips to the top and bottom of the block. The quilt top should measure 22½" square, including seam allowances.

2. Position five reverse-appliquéd border scallops on a white 4½"-wide strip, making sure to leave at least ¼" beyond the scallops on all sides. Stitch the scallops in place. Make four strips.

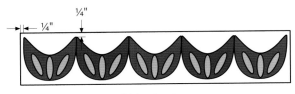

Make 4 strips,
4½" × 22½".

3. Sew two of the appliquéd strips to opposite sides of the quilt top, making sure to orient the strips as shown in the quilt assembly diagram below. Sew a white 4½" square to each end of the two remaining appliquéd strips and sew them to the top and bottom of the quilt top. The quilt top should measure 30½" square.

Quilt assembly

Finishing the Quilt

For more details on the following finishing steps, visit ShopMartingale.com/HowtoQuilt for free downloadable information.

1. Layer the quilt top with batting and backing; baste the layers together.

2. Quilt by hand or machine. The quilt shown is machine quilted in the ditch and then a feather and pebble design is free-motion quilted in the quilt center and outer border. A scalloped line is quilted throughout the inner border.

3. Using the blue print 2¼"-wide strips, make binding and then attach the binding to the quilt.

> Appliqué patterns do not include seam allowances.

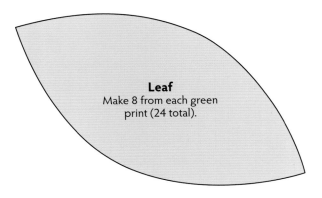

Leaf
Make 8 from each green print (24 total).

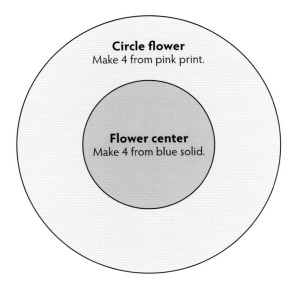

Circle flower
Make 4 from pink print.

Flower center
Make 4 from blue solid.

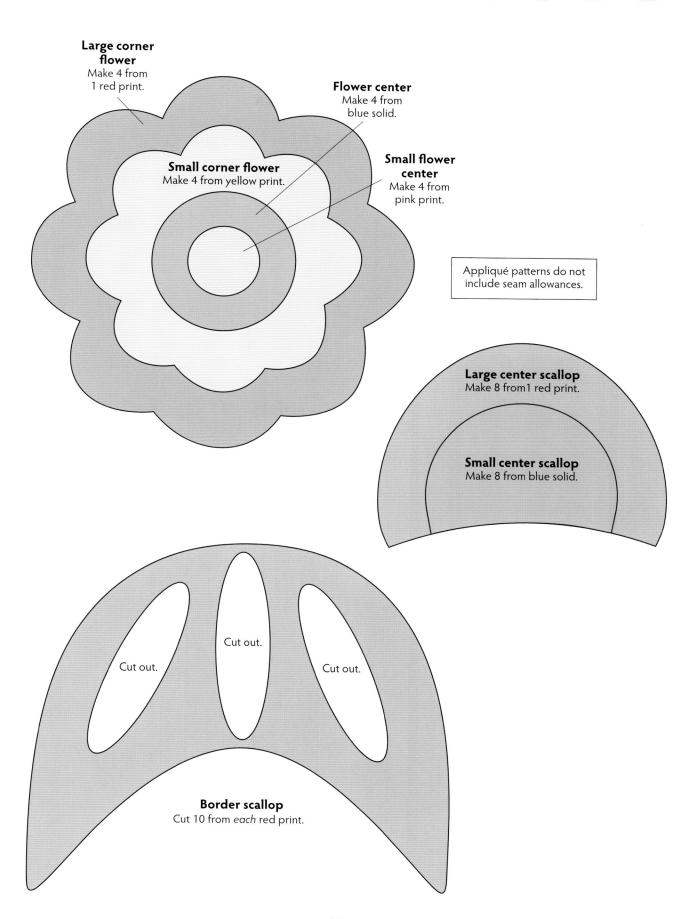

Large corner flower
Make 4 from 1 red print.

Flower center
Make 4 from blue solid.

Small corner flower
Make 4 from yellow print.

Small flower center
Make 4 from pink print.

Appliqué patterns do not include seam allowances.

Large center scallop
Make 8 from1 red print.

Small center scallop
Make 8 from blue solid.

Cut out.

Cut out.

Cut out.

Border scallop
Cut 10 from *each* red print.

Appliqué patterns do not include seam allowances. When cutting out ovals, be sure to leave a narrow seam allowance for turning under.

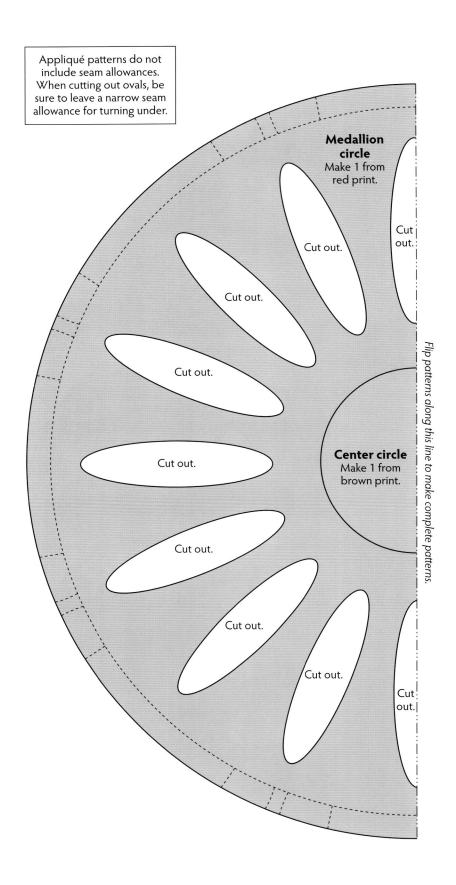

Medallion circle
Make 1 from red print.

Cut out.

Cut out.

Cut out.

Cut out.

Cut out.

Cut out.

Cut out.

Center circle
Make 1 from brown print.

Cut out.

Cut out.

Cut out.

Cut out.

Cut out.

Flip patterns along this line to make complete patterns.

Fabric Selection

I enjoy using as many fabrics as I can in my quilts, but the selection process isn't random. After choosing an overall color palette, such as red, blue, and green, I start pulling fabrics of each color from my fabric stash. If I'm using red, not all reds in my stash are the same color or tone. So I start by pulling out all the red fabrics to see my options. Then I narrow the selection to the red tones I want to use, such as cherry red or tomato red. I use the same method for the background fabrics, selecting a range of tone on tones that go well together. I don't use large amounts of any one fabric—typically only about ½ yard. If I run short on one fabric, I can easily add another in the same color or tone.

Another way I choose fabrics is to mix up the prints within each color selection, being sure to include small-, medium-, and large-scale prints as well as dots, stripes, plaids, and florals. Using fabrics in this way gives quilts more dimension and interest.

Machine Appliqué

M y love for appliqué started with my very first quilt. Over my quilting lifetime I have tried many ways to appliqué and have taken the parts of each technique that I like and developed methods that suit my style. Described in this section are the two main methods I use to prepare appliqué shapes for stitching: freezer paper and wash-away appliqué paper. I use each method for different reasons, finding it's sometimes necessary to combine techniques to get the best results.

For either preparation method you can sew the appliqués by hand or by machine to give the look of hand-sewn appliqué. My personal preference is invisible machine stitching, because:

◆ Machine stitching is strong, even, and secure.

◆ When using monofilament or fine polyester thread, the stitches are truly invisible.

◆ Stitching the appliqués by machine is quicker than sewing them by hand. Time is precious because I have many quilts I want to make and many more ideas for new designs.

Tools

The tools listed below are what I use to create perfect turned-edge invisible machine appliqué.

◆ Freezer paper

◆ Wash-away appliqué paper (also called wash-away appliqué sheets)

◆ Sharp fabric scissors with micro-serrated blades

◆ Paper scissors

◆ Pointed tailor's awl

◆ Cuticle stick

◆ Small stencil brush, ¼" diameter

◆ Transparent tracing paper

◆ Flower-head pins

◆ Microtex Sharp machine needles, size 60/8

◆ Polyester thread: monofilament in smoke or clear OR 100-weight polyester (Invisifil or MicroQuilter) in a range of colors to match the appliqué pieces

◆ Cotton or polyester thread, 60-weight, to match the background fabric

◆ Water-soluble basting glue (I prefer Roxanne's Glue-Baste-It)

◆ Acid-free, water-soluble glue stick or glue pen

◆ Stapler

◆ Small iron

◆ Fine mechanical pencil

◆ Bias-tape maker, sizes ¼" and ½"

◆ Sewing machine in good working order with a zigzag stitch for which the width and length can be adjusted. Being able to move the needle position is also helpful, but not necessary.

Method 1: Freezer Paper

When it comes to appliquéing borders or large parts of the quilt center, I prefer to use freezer-paper templates. That way I don't need to wash the quilt or appliqué block when it's finished. For this method, the appliqué pattern doesn't need to be reversed.

Preparing the Templates

The finished template must have smoothly cut edges to ensure great-looking appliqué shapes. The finished appliqué shapes will look exactly like the freezer-paper template.

1 Place freezer paper, dull side up, over each pattern piece and trace exactly on the lines using a fine mechanical pencil. Do not add a seam allowance. Mark

any areas that will lie underneath another shape with a dashed line. Use paper scissors to roughly cut out each freezer-paper template.

2 To save time when many pieces are required, cut up to six pieces of freezer paper and stack them dull side up. Place the roughly cut template on top of the stack. Anchor the layers together using staples or pins. Cut out the pattern pieces on the drawn line. To achieve smooth pattern edges, move the paper, rather than the scissors, as you take long cutting strokes.

3 Repeat steps 1 and 2, making one freezer-paper template for each appliqué shape in the quilt. If you remove them carefully, you can reuse the templates several times. This is helpful when making multiple blocks with repeated appliqué shapes.

Preparing the Fabric Shapes

Before cutting your fabric, press it so it's wrinkle-free.

1 Use flower-head pins to pin freezer-paper templates, shiny side *up*, to the wrong side of the fabric, leaving at least ½" between each shape for seam allowances. Place the templates so that the longest lines

or curves of each shape are on the diagonal or bias, which will make it easier to press the seam allowances over the template.

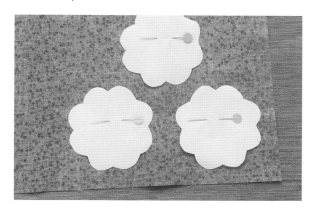

2 Using fabric scissors, cut out each fabric shape, adding a generous ¼" seam allowance. A generous seam allowance is best, as you can always trim any seam allowance that feels too bulky.

3 For inner points, make one clip at the center position, stopping two or three threads from the edge of the template. It may be necessary to make a small clip on each side of the center clip.

Machine Appliqué

4 Clip inner curves, stopping three or four threads from the edge of the template. The larger the curve, the more clips are needed. For small, tight inner curves, cut two small V shapes.

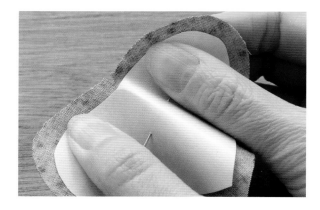

5 Use the point of an awl or seam ripper to fold the seam allowance over onto the shiny side of the freezer-paper template. Hold a hot, dry iron on the seam allowance and use the heat to seal the fabric to the shiny side of the template. When you've pressed enough of the seam allowance to anchor the fabric in place, remove the pin. Clips made in the curves and inner points will aid in turning the seam allowance. Do not fold over any seam allowances that will lie underneath another shape.

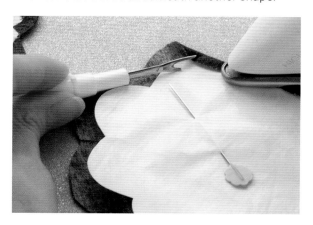

Preparing Leaves and Circles

1 As described in "Preparing the Fabric Shapes" on page 73, pin a freezer-paper template, with the shiny side *up,* to the wrong side of the fabric.

2 For leaves and other pieces with outer points, fold one edge of the fabric shape over the freezer-paper template, extending the fold beyond the point of the template. Fold the other side in the same way. Remove the pin when you've pressed enough of the seam allowance to anchor the fabric in place.

3 If you have a little fabric "flag" sticking out, use the point of an awl to fold the flag behind the point. Using a little water and a small stencil brush, dab the flag with water, making sure to dampen only the fabric, *not* the freezer-paper template. Press using a hot iron. Repeat as needed to complete the leaf shape.

Flag

4 For circles, use a hot, dry iron and the tip of an awl or seam ripper to fold the seam allowance over the freezer-paper template. Use the awl to keep the seam allowance lying firmly against the edge of the circle template, slightly gathering the seam allowance as you go, being careful not to distort the template. Working a little bit (about ½") at a time, use the side of your iron to achieve smooth edges and adhere the seam allowance to the template. Remove the pin when you've pressed enough of the seam allowance to anchor the fabric in place.

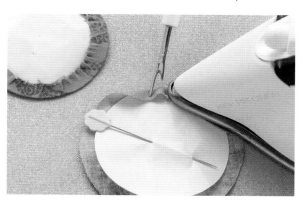

Method 2: Wash–Away Appliqué Paper

This method works well for tricky curves, small circles, and reverse appliqué.

1 For this method, any asymmetrical patterns need to be reversed before cutting the templates. See "Reversing the Patterns" below. Place a sheet of wash-away appliqué paper, dull side *up*, over each pattern piece. Trace exactly on the lines using a fine mechanical pencil. Do not add a seam allowance. Mark any areas that lie underneath another shape with a dashed line. Use paper scissors to cut out each template directly on the line.

Reversing the Patterns

To make a reverse image, trace the entire appliqué pattern onto a piece of plain paper. Then place the paper on a light box or against a bright window, with the traced side toward the light. Trace the shape onto the back of the paper using a black permanent pen.

2 Place the templates so that the longest lines or curves of each shape are on the diagonal or bias, which will make it easier to press the seam allowances over the template. Fuse each template to the wrong side of the fabric, following the manufacturer's instructions.

3 Referring to steps 2–4 of "Preparing the Fabric Shapes" on page 73, cut out each shape, adding a generous ¼" seam allowance. Clip the curves and inner points as needed.

4 Use a fabric glue stick or glue pen to apply glue to the seam allowance. (Glue is blue in photo, but it dries clear.) Use an awl to fold the seam allowances over onto the template. Do not fold over any seam allowances that will lie underneath another appliqué shape.

Preparing Stems and Vines

To prepare stems and vines, I use a ¼" or ½" bias-tape maker, depending on the size of the stem or vine in the quilt. Using a bias-tape maker gives me a perfectly even stem or vine that lies flat beneath the other appliqué shapes.

If the stem or vine needs to curve, you will need to cut the fabric on the bias. If the stem or vine is straight, I cut them on the straight of grain. If you are using fabric that won't hold a crease well, lightly spray your strips with starch before placing them in the bias-tape maker.

When using the bias-tape maker, cut fabric strips double the width of the bias-tape maker. For example, for a ¼" bias-tape maker, cut strips ½" wide by the length needed.

1 Using a long rotary-cutting ruler, line up the 45° angle with the edge of the fabric. Cut along the edge of the ruler and discard the smaller piece. Cut the number of bias strips needed in the required width for the project you are making. If cutting straight-of-grain strips, cut the number of strips needed in the required width across the width of the fabric.

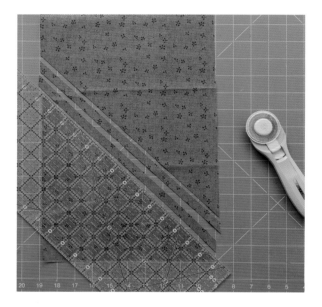

2 If using straight-of-grain strips, cut one end of the strip at a 45° angle. (Bias strips will already have an angled end.) Place the angled end into the bias-tape maker as shown. Pull just the tip of the strip through the device.

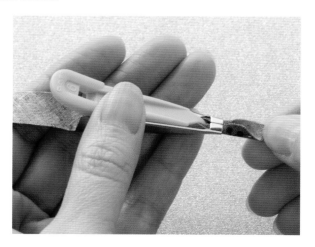

Cutting Bias Strips

To make cutting bias strips easier, I start by cutting a 10"- or 20"-wide strip across the width of the fabric. The width of the fabric strip depends on whether I'm making short stems or longer vines, but with either width all the bias-cut strips will be the same length. It's always better for the strips to be a little longer than needed. A 10"-wide fabric strip will yield 14"-long bias strips. A 20"-wide strip will yield bias strips that are approximately 28" long. The number of bias strips you can cut depends on their width.

3 Using a hot iron and steam, place the tip of your iron on the tip of the fabric. Gently pull the bias-tape maker slowly along the strip, following closely behind with the iron to crease the edges of the strip as it emerges from the device. Lay the strip flat and press from the right side to finish.

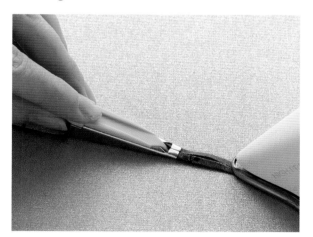

Preparing Your Sewing Machine

Monofilament (clear nylon thread) is a good choice for machine appliqué because it's truly forgiving. If your machine has trouble with monofilament, try 100-weight polyester thread in colors that match the appliqué fabrics. When using polyester thread, you need to stay very close to the edge of the appliqué pieces to prevent the thread from showing on the background fabric.

1 Use a size 60/8 needle in your sewing machine and thread it with monofilament or 100-weight polyester thread.

2 Wind the bobbin with 60-weight cotton or polyester thread. Reduce the top tension.

Tension Reduction

Because monofilament tends to stretch a little, the top tension needs to be reduced. The tension setting will vary depending on your machine. Start by setting the tension to 3.0. Test the stitch on a scrap of fabric. If the bobbin thread is visible on the top, reduce the tension and test the stitch again. Continue in the same way until the bobbin thread is not visible on the top.

3 Use an open-toe embroidery foot and set the machine to the zigzag stitch. Shorten the stitch length to approximately ⅛" or 1.6 mm. Adjust the stitch width to between 0.3 and 0.8 mm, so the inner stitches land two or three threads inside the appliqué and the outer stitches pierce the background immediately next to the appliqué.

Additional Settings

If invisible machine appliqué is new to you, start with a slightly wider stitch. As you become more comfortable, you can make the stitches narrower. My zigzag stitch is so narrow, it looks more like a crooked straight stitch. Once the tension setting, stitch width, and stitch length are the way I want them, I program the stitch into the memory of my machine. You can also simply write down the settings on a piece of paper. If your machine has a speed-control feature, set it to a slower speed. Sewing slowly allows you to make smaller stitches. A hover function for the presser foot, as well as a knee lift to raise the presser foot, are both helpful, as they make it easier to pivot the fabric with the needle in the down position while sewing curves.

4 If possible, move the needle to the far right so that you can align the inside of the presser foot with the edge of the appliqué. If you cannot change the needle position, align the edge of the appliqué with the center of the presser foot as shown below.

Stitching the Appliqués

When stitching by machine, I find it's helpful to use a stabilizer such as freezer paper or wash-away appliqué paper to give the appliqué pieces a firm edge and to avoid stretching and distortion.

1 Use the needle up/down button or the machine's flywheel to pull the bobbin thread up to the top. Holding onto the threads, start by taking three or four small straight stitches in the background fabric to lock the threads in place.

2 Carefully stitch around each appliqué shape, starting with the bottom layer. To maintain good control, sew at a slow to moderate speed, stopping and pivoting as often as needed to keep the edge of your shape in the correct position.

3 To firmly secure an inner or outer point, stitch exactly to the point and then stop with the needle down. Pivot the fabric and continue stitching along the next side of the shape.

4 Continue stitching around the edge of the appliqué until you come to the starting point. End with three to four small straight stitches in the background fabric.

5 For "Method 1: Freezer Paper" (page 72), slit the background fabric underneath the appliqué with scissors, being careful not to cut the appliqué fabric. Trim the background fabric, leaving a generous ¼" seam allowance. Using a cuticle stick, gently remove the freezer-paper template. Be sure to remove the template before stitching any overlapping layers (see "Building Appliqué Units" below).

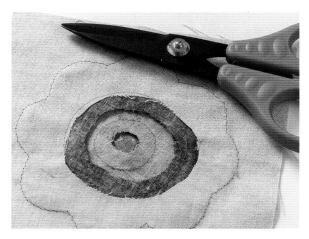

6 For "Method 2: Wash-Away Appliqué Paper" (page 75), after appliqué is complete, gently wash each block in cool water to remove the basting glue and soften the appliqué paper. Lay the block flat on a towel to dry. Gently press the block, wrong side up, on top of a towel. Once dry, trim the block to the correct measurement.

Building Appliqué Units

When multiple appliqué shapes are layered on top of one another, such as in a rose, it's easiest to join the layers first and then stitch the completed unit to the background. This method is particularly helpful when appliquéing borders or large areas of the quilt, because it reduces the times you'll need to turn the quilt top.

1 Use either of the two appliqué methods to prepare the appliqué shapes. For this example, I used "Method 1: Freezer Paper" (page 72) and the patterns for Goose Crossing on page 47.

2 Pin or glue baste a small circle on top of a larger circle. Referring to steps 1–4 of "Stitching the Appliqués" on page 78, stitch around the small circle using a tiny zigzag stitch. If you're making more than one unit, you can chain piece the units. To chain piece, don't cut the thread when you're finished sewing one unit, just move on to the next unit.

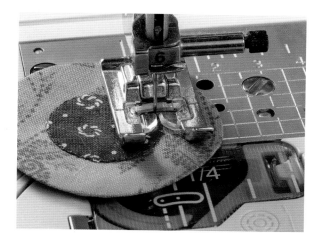

3 Remove the freezer-paper template from inside the small stitched circle only. Do not remove the template beyond the stitched line. If the seam allowance on the large circle is coming loose, use a dry iron to press it back in place. If you used "Method 2: Wash-Away Appliqué Paper" to prepare the appliqué shapes, skip to step 5 since you do not need to remove the template.

4 Carefully trim away the fabric only inside the stitched circle, adding a ¼" seam allowance, to reveal the small circle template. Remove the freezer-paper template

from the small circle as described in step 5 of "Stitching the Appliqués."

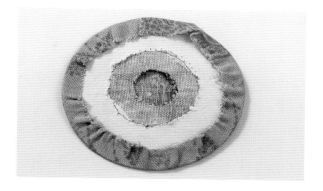

5 Pin or glue baste the two-circle unit onto the larger flower. Stitch in place using a small zigzag stitch.

6 For "Method 1: Freezer Paper," repeat steps 3 and 4 to remove the freezer-paper template from the center of the circle unit only.

7 Stitch the flower appliqué to the background fabric using the small zigzag stitch. Trim away the background fabric under the flower, leaving ¼" seam allowance. Remove the remaining freezer paper.

About the Author

I grew up in a family of makers in rural New Zealand. Every item of clothing I owned (and I had many) was made by my mother, from pretty dresses to beautifully knitted jumpers. At five years old I had enough dresses to wear a different one each day for two weeks, but I had a favorite! It was mauve with a row of pussycats along the bottom and I wanted to wear it every day. My older sister had the hard job of persuading me to wear a different dress.

Sewing days were special and very dear to my heart. We lived out in the country on a dairy farm, so going to town was a real treat. The first shop my mum would go to was the fabric shop, where we were allowed to choose the fabric for ourselves. When we got home my mother, sister, and I would spend the days in Mum's sewing room making our creations.

Mum was a dressmaker by trade and a perfectionist, and she could make anything. I would often see an outfit in a magazine, and she would make it for me. My grandmother, also a maker, taught me the arts of knitting and crochet. I loved spending time with her while she sat with her crochet hook making fine doilies, bedspreads, and knitted garments that she sold.

All of this early introduction to the world of fabric and threads led me to who I am today; making quilts was truly a destiny just waiting for me around the corner. As a mother of two grown sons and wife of a busy man living on a small farm overlooking New Zealand's Kaipara Harbour, I have time to create my own quilt designs that express my love of vintage and reproduction fabrics. Visit my website, www.sharonkeightleyquilts.com.